Ruramai Nyadzayo Mugwisi

# A Seed in The Dust

## an African Memoir

Foreword by Rebecca Kanoerera;
Host 'Rebecca Talks"

**Wholeness**
Incorporated
Publishing

*This book is dedicated to You...*
*May you find courage and hope*
*and always know that you are the*
*miracle...*

Ruramai Nyadzayo Mugwisi

# A Seed in The Dust

## an African Memoir

# CONTENTS

# FOREWORD

It was a chance and yet so fitting encounter with Ruramai Nyadzayo-Mugwisi at a High Tea women's event which was being hosted and attended by some incredibly talented Zimbabwean business women. I remember that beautiful day, we had both arrived early for the event and took advantage of the time to strike poses in our beautiful outfits. In the process of networking, we found we had stories to share, dreams to pursue and from that day on we became cheerleaders to each other. As an author, coach, trainer and talk show host I believe in the power of storytelling. I am an avid reader, and once my hands get a hold of a good book, I find it hard to put it down, because I get consumed in the journey of the characters. The book, A Seed in The Dust; An African Memoir grabbed my attention and I was hooked from the very first page to the last. I drank in every last drop of each word, which was creatively placed on every sentence, paragraph, and chapter. I paused at each comma and took a deep breath after the full stops. An emotional roller coaster, with hard truths of the realities of a beautiful strong female character who indeed was thrown to the ground repeatedly. She had some beautiful exhilarating moments of her becoming an independent woman. The drama, the characters, the tears, the joys and the pain. Ruramai is not silent about some of the issues faced in today's society that are kept behind closed doors. She is so descriptive in her storytelling that I could feel the emotions, smell, hear the sounds and see the colours of the settings in Zimbabwe where this story was vividly set from. My prayer is for the readers to be inspired and moved to dust themselves off from any situation that may have pushed them down, to find a voice where they have been silenced, to find peace and healing from any hurt and pain, and to never give up on the power of a seed that will keep rising to its full potential. Thank you Ruramai for writing this book as a gift to many who need reminding to have hope, faith even as small as a mustard seed and to love themselves enough to not allow any situation or person to crush their spirit.

REBECCA KANOERERA
—HOST "REBECCA TALKS"

# INTRODUCTION

I have fought battles that left me bleeding and gasping for air while I relentlessly held on but I was not always this brave and fearless. I am human after all. I have given up and surrendered many times, all the fight in me gone. We all have scars from traumas and trials we would rather forget. In the aftermath of my pain I thought I would never be whole again, that I would never heal. Yet I still breathe, alive and healing. I say healing because I know the journey is not over. Not by a long shot. There will be other battles but today I am here in this place, somewhere between thankful and hopeful. I am grateful to be alive. The future beckons and I am excited and hopeful about the prospects which lie ahead. The undeniable truth is that I have come a long way from the little lost girl of the past. One halting step at a time, often times those steps leading to dark and unfamiliar places. Sometimes it feels as though I've lived an eternity in these 44 years of life I've traversed through time; a lifetime of lost hope, broken dreams, restoration, compassion and love.

I look outside the window at the darkening horizon. Thick black clouds are gathering in the sky where the sun was shining just a few hours before. The smell of rain fills my nostrils and I smile. I love the rain. I envisage the raindrops gently falling on the muddy brown earth giving life to a budding fragile shoot emerging from the darkness beneath the ground. There is an unexpected beauty in the broken. Like the grace in the curve of a flower pummelled by the wind almost to snapping point. In my own life, I have been buffeted by the relentless stormy winds of fear, shame and rejection. I too have been broken like the flower, petals drifting into the dark that surrounds me. But like a seed I have emerged from the darkness, reborn and willing to try again.

The rain heralds a new season of growth and promise. New seasons are exciting and challenging, requiring from us courage and the tenacity to gracefully face the inevitable discomfort of change. The old has to make way for the new and we look forward to the novelty of the new in our lives but embracing the struggle of adapting to the healing that must first take place in order to move forward is seldom easy. To anticipate and discern the unfolding of new possibilities in the crises and calamities we face as the seasons change is a gift we all must possess. If we would look more closely we would see that our lives are filled with new promise at every turn even in seasons which bring uncertainty and fear.

NEW SEASONS ARE EXCITING AND CHALLENGING, REQUIRING FROM US COURAGE AND THE TENACITY TO GRACEFULLY FACE THE INEVITABLE DISCOMFORT OF CHANGE.

I recently embarked on a new adventure. I can never stay in one place for too long. There are always more hands needed to be of service somewhere in this vast global space we call home. The gospel of Matthew in the thirty seventh verse of the 9th chapter captures the essence of a service centred life: 'The harvest is great but the workers are few.' I am a Christian as you can tell but my story is not about religious conversion as much as it is about holding onto faith in impossible situations regardless of religion. Without faith we are all adrift and in danger of sinking in an abyss of hopelessness and self-destruction. Without faith I would not be alive to narrate this story.

It has been two months since I packed my bags and moved to

another country. After more than a decade of building a legacy of hope and restoration in the land of my birth I uprooted myself from the comfort of familiar surroundings in pursuit of new possibilities. I do not have all the answers but I do have my voice. I use my voice to share my story in the hopes that it will remind all of us why we are here and most importantly why we live. Often times discovering the reason why we are, propels us on a journey into healing, transformation and purpose. The journey is messy, uncomfortable and distressing. Coming face to face with our deepest yearnings intertwined with our deepest pain is unsettling and unnerving. Our hearts would rather forget and so we master the art of hiding our wounds and scars.

Zuva meaning sunshine in the Shona dialect is an apt description for my own life. My life has weathered many storms and the horizon is filled with yet more dark clouds but the sunshine has continued to shine in the midst of the upheaval and despair. The storm is a vehicle of my growth. It is in the midst of the storm that I discover my capacity to withstand adversity. Without the storm I would never be aware of the strength and grace within me. I admit it is not easy to remain courageous when catastrophe calls but it is the assurance that when it is all over I will be stronger than I was before that makes me realise that no battle is wasted. Even the ones I walk away from feeling I lost everything. Everything ultimately works out for good. That is why I still love the sound of rain and I am not afraid of storms. I can hear thunder rumbling in the distance. A storm is coming but first let me start my story from the beginning.

# FAITH

"SHIPS IN HARBOUR
ARE SAFE, BUT
THAT'S NOT WHAT
SHIPS ARE BUILT
FOR."

(JOHN SHEDD)

# CHAPTER 1

I was always inquisitive and curious, which quickly earned me the label of being too liberal and independent at an early age. Born in an era where children were expected to be seen more than they were heard, my behaviour came to be regarded as outlandish and inappropriate. I had many questions, enough to fill a book my mother often exclaimed in exasperation. Staring at the star strewn sky on balmy evenings when we sat outside I wondered why moonlit nights did not burn as bright as sun-filled days even though both moon and sun hung in the same sky to give light. Watching my grandmother carefully select herbs to chew for a toothache, I reflected on how it came to be revealed which root could heal and which herb could kill, did someone have to die to make it known. I voiced these questions aloud and found it perplexing that my curiosity elicited more frustration and annoyance than answers.

"You ask too many questions!"

"What is wrong with you? Why can't you be like other children!" were the irate responses I often received to my questions. I knew even at that young age that I could not be like everybody else because I was exactly who I was! I wondered why anybody would want me to be an exact replica of another. Were they like everybody else too? Sharing the same thoughts, dreams and lives? Like my grandfather's sheep. Each white furry, bleating sheep looked each alike, from one to the next and they behaved just the same. I could not be like my grandfather's sheep and I made every effort to seek the answers which could serve my curiosity on my own. It was this curiosity which set in motion the steps which led me to a heart wrenching and yet life fulfilling destiny that was far greater than I had ever envisioned.

It all began in the year 1977. I was born in the unrecognised Republic of Rhodesia (later known as Zimbabwe) at a time when oppression and exploitation melded into hope and freedom. Oppression of a people denied full citizen rights in their ancestral land amidst the upheaval of a liberation war which had taken its staggering toll on both warring parties. Hope and freedom as the war ended and peace emerged, faltering and shaky but peace nevertheless. In 1980, three years after I was born Zimbabwe finally attained her independence. Freedom was no longer a political idea to fan the flames of a brutal war which had raged on for more than a decade, now a dawning possibility. Freedom, no longer a prayer and a hope for a people cowered into submission and fear through years of repressive colonial rule but finally a reality.

Freedom hung in the air, infused in the palpable joy and smiles of the people. Freedom was in the rhythmic beat of the township music blaring out of the dusty storefronts of the local shops. Freedom was almost tangible and within reach as each man and woman could now determine his or her own destiny without fear of reprisal from an oppressive government. Parents could plan a better future for their children. Young people could finally study for careers that would propel them to work in hallways and offices which once housed only people of a certain race. Opportunity was synonymous with freedom.

My father was part of the history which shaped the freedom and opportunity that became my reality growing up. Brian Kawa was a passionate man driven into the political fray of the conflict playing out in the countryside and along the borders of the country. He left for

Mozambique at the age of 17 and had taken up arms to challenge the authority of the colonial government. Periodically he secretly re-entered the country to canvas for resources and support to sustain the liberation war effort on the frontline. During these risky jaunts back home he was based in a small farming town close to the border east of the capital city. This location provided quick access to a number of farmers sympathetic to the cause of the war, who in turn pledged food and clothing that fed the liberation war army living in the caves and hills tucked away in the rolling plains of the surrounding region. It was in Marondera that he met my mother.

Emilia Kawa was a diminutive woman with big dreams. Raised by a father who did not believe in educating daughters because as my grandfather often said when he was drunk from the locally brewed intoxicating mash that was his favourite pastime, "*Kudzidzisa musikana kupedza pfuma*". (Educating a girl is a waste of money)'. "Daughters are only good for the bride price they bring when they reach a marriageable age" he would add. Therefore, my grandfather paid school fees for his daughters to attain only the elementary level of education. High school education was the preserve of the male lineage in the family. My mother did not let this deter her.

My mother was not one to passively let things happen. Instead of giving up she defiantly decided she would acquire an education with or without my grandfather's support. She enlisted the help of her teachers and forged an agreement with the local high school to attend classes during the term and to work for her tuition fees during the school holidays. It was a situation fraught with great difficulty which demanded a delicate balance of her time and attention between her school obligations and the responsibilities required of a good daughter at home. Many of those responsibilities were quietly shouldered by my grandmother. While appearing to demurely acquiesce to her husband's traditional demands my grandmother enabled her tenacious daughter to fulfil her dream of acquiring an education My mother's tenacity paid off and she qualified as a nurse in 1965.

My father had a self-assured and easy way about him that dissipated a brooding, hidden intensity he usually kept under restraint. His charm lay in his quick smile and quiet nature and it was this ease that drew in others around him making them comfortable in his presence. Underlying his friendly demeanour was a

> WHILE APPEARING TO DEMURELY ACQUIESCE TO HER HUSBAND'S TRADITIONAL DEMANDS MY GRANDMOTHER ENABLED HER TENACIOUS DAUGHTER TO FULFIL HER DREAM OF ACQUIRING AN EDUCATION.

compelling depth of intelligence and drive and it was this relentless ambition that piqued my mother's interest when she first met him. Their courtship was short because circumstances necessitated expediency even in matters of the heart. They were married in a simple ceremony in 1967 at my grandfather's homestead. A year later my sister Rose was born and my father left for Mozambique soon after. He did not return until 8 years later. This was the longest he had ever been away from home on his secret excursions into the battlefield.

I was their second child, born nine years after my sister Rose was born. My father had left for the battlefront again only this time he had been assigned to travel to Zambia and he was stationed there for about 4 months by the time she went into labour. After a difficult delivery; my mother was in labour for 60 hours because the only doctor resident at the rural hospital run by Christian missionaries was not available as he had travelled to attend to pressing family matters. The doctor returned two days later and I was born by Caesarean section and I was taken home by my grandmother two days later while my mother was detained in hospital for a further two weeks due to severe post-delivery complications. I was regarded as a special miracle and upon arrival from the hospital after my birth it is said that my mother's brother, Uncle Francis took one look at me and proclaimed '*Shumirai Mwari!* (Worship God!') and from that day I was named Shumirai. During those two weeks I was fed watered down goats' milk until my mother was given a clean bill of health and she returned home to nurse me much to the relief of my grandmother who had become my primary caregiver.

My mother nursed me for the first two months of my life but she soon had to return to work and a decision was made to leave me in the immediate care of my grandmother. I loved my grandmother, Gogo as I called her as I grew up and she soon became a mother to me. I forged an inextricable bond with my Uncle Francis who was very protective over me and he became a father figure in my life. I lived with my grandparents and uncle until I turned four. I have a sparse recollection of the infant years of my life. My earliest memory of my childhood in rural Masvingo is of Gogo and Uncle Francis. One particular memory stands out. Uncle Francis was teaching me to float in the river which streamed behind our homestead when I was almost four years old. My arms flailing wildly, I screamed in terror as the dark waters rushed over my head as a heavy weight seemed to drag me down to the murky depths of the river. Suddenly gasping for air I felt a tug on my ankle as Uncle Francis plucked me out of the water. His hand had never lost its tight grip on me.

"I have you Shumirai" he murmured as he pacified me. It was Uncle Francis who eventually taught me how to swim. My grandmother told me how I became an avid swimmer by the time I had to leave her and join my parents and my sister Rose. I was four when I had to leave my Gogo and Uncle Francis to go and live with my family in Marondera. I cried inconsolably when Gogo told me that I would be living in Marondera. My mother had returned to Masvingo to take me home. I did not want to leave Gogo and my dear Uncle Francis. She consoled me as she told me about my sister Rose and my father who had returned home after the war. She told me that I would be very happy there. We were going to be a family.

# CHAPTER 2

What is the meaning of this?'
My mother stood in the doorway to the girl's bedroom visibly angered, glowering at me as I sat on the bed where a moment ago I had been giggling with my cousin Faith. There was no mistaking that angry glint in her eyes. She was in a towering rage. Faith stood up as if to leave the room but Mama stood resolutely in the doorway, blocking her only way out. We all knew how uncomfortable it was to witness my mother's ireful reaction to anybody she perceived as being disobedient and nobody wanted to be caught in the cross hairs of a falling out with her. These encounters usually ended in tears for the one caught on the wrong side of the contention. My mother's tongue was as unapologetically forthright as it was sharp. Her incisive words could cut through the toughest façade. An uneasy silence filled the room. I lowered my gaze as my mind raced trying to recollect what I could have possibly done that had incensed her to this degree.

'Look at me when I am speaking to you Shumi!' she snapped.

Slowly I raised my eyes to meet her penetrating gaze and then I noticed something in her hands. She was holding a small reed shopping basket woven with blue ribbon on the handles which I had just brought in minutes earlier from the errand I had been sent on to go to the butchery. Suddenly I knew why she was angry and my heart plummeted in fear.

After the war had ended, we had moved to the capital city of Harare with the aim of enabling my father to obtain a job in the city. Greater opportunities existed for employment in the city than in the small farming town of Marondera where he had returned to live with my mother after the declaration of the ceasefire between the two warring parties; the freedom fighters and the minority white-led government. My parents and my sister Rose had lived in Marondera until a year after independence was declared in 1980 when I had joined them. With a stroke of luck my father found a job as a salesman in a motor spares company after the manager of the company decided to go out on a limb for a promising young veteran from the war. My father's quick wit, quiet charm as well as the invaluable administrative skills gleaned from his war time background made up for the lack of academic credentials on his application. The gamble paid off handsomely for both the manager as well as my father. Evidently my father was in his element in this position and soon the large commissions he made from successful sales enabled him to buy our own home, albeit a humble one but still our very own home.

Three years later my father had lost his job when the motor spares company embarked on a human resource drive that saw them employ newly graduated students from the big university in the city. My father armed with only his beguiling charm was outmatched by their complex business language and even more impressive academic performance. His pride devastated by the loss of his job he now spent more time drinking at the local tavern.

Our home was in Chitungwiza, a sprawling suburb south-east of the city of Harare established for low to middle income earners. Built in the colonial era for the black working class who made their way to the nearby manufacturing factories which spewed black smoke along the main highway that led into the city which was an hour's drive away, it was packed with identical square houses that looked like matchstick boxes from a distance. It was a modest home with 4 rooms; two bedrooms, a small corner room that passed as a living room and an even smaller kitchen that could barely contain 3 people at a time. The bathroom was a single outbuilding adjacent to the entrance of our home which housed a toilet seat on one side and a shiny shower head on the opposite wall. My mother prided herself on keeping a clean home and our home gleamed and sparkled from hours of rigorous cleaning with soapy water that reminded me of lemons and oranges in the summer.

My mother had found a position as a nurse at the big hospital in the city. She would leave for work very early in the morning in her spotless white uniform with glistening epaulettes and buttons. She looked the very picture of professional capability. It was very important work for a village girl who had lived all her life in small farming towns. She could finally practise all elements of emergency medicine that she had only read about in textbooks in a fully equipped city hospital. Added to that was the bonus of a higher income awarded to city nurses and my mother now earned enough to support the large extended family that was always coming to the city looking for help; financial or otherwise.

Our home was always bustling with activity largely from visiting cousins, aunts and uncles from either side of my parent's families who often came with various pleas for assistance. Their requests varied from seed for the next planting season to clothing, food or medicine for headaches, colds or a myriad of other common ailments. The older aunts and uncles would visit routinely for a week or two before departing for their homes after their requests were fulfilled. The younger relatives, who were more often teenage cousins, usually stayed longer in the hope of finding jobs in the nearby factories or places to study in the black owned vocational colleges that were sprouting up on the out-skirts of the city.

I revelled in the constant stream of visiting people in our home, basking in the attention I received. I was 7 years old and the newest addition to our family, my sister Tinashe was only a few months old. The last seven years of ruling the house as the youngest one were suddenly over. My mother's attention was divided between the demands of the new baby and running the busy household. I was not particularly close to my mother and although I did not understand why our relationship was strained initially, I realised as I grew older that perhaps there was a part of me that resented Mama for choosing to leave me while she lived with Rose in the early years of my life. I loved Mama but I still regarded Gogo as my natural mother. I was drawn to my father's enigmatic aura and we spent many evenings in animated story telling as he regaled me with folk tales from when he was growing up, but since he had lost his job he was spending less and less time at home. I ached for the love and attention I used to receive before he started unravelling after he lost his job. Feeling lost and neglected I turned to the comfort of my visiting cousins for attention. I captivated them with my quirky personality and even more fascinating stories and I was soon firmly established as the funny and bubbly cousin who also had a penchant for drama and a streak of naughtiness that was harmless usually. Harmless until that Saturday morning when my mother stood in the doorway to the bedroom I shared with my sister Rose and two other cousins holding the shopping basket in her hands.

Mama would send us to Mr. Moyo's butchery every Saturday morning to buy our weekly order for meat. Mr. Moyo supplied all cuts of meat-rump steak, tender sirloin and chuck beef for stewing (which was my favourite because I would suck on the meaty bones in my mother's full flavoured hearty beef stew mixed with vegetables;

carrots, potatoes, sugar beans and spinach). My mother believed in instilling independence and responsibility in children from an early age and she had assigned weekly shopping duties for my sister Rose who was now 16 years old, my two cousins Faith and Precious who were both 15 years old and after three supervised trips at 7 years of age I had recently started going on unsupervised shopping trips to the butchery.

Mr. Moyo's butchery was right at the end of the shopping complex, next to MS Superette, a convenience shop which sold tea, sugar, bread and jam. The shopping complex was a short walk away from home which took me through the narrow winding streets of Chitungwiza and right past the house my friend Dora's family shared with another family. The butchery had a reinforced glass door with a steel frame that opened into a spotless interior with glistening glass topped cabinets running the length of the room in the middle of the butchery. Stainless steel counter tops covered the glass encased cabinets sectioned along one wall of the room and beneath one of these counters was a wooden cash box from which dangled a formidable padlock. Mr Moyo kept the key on a bronze chain dangling from a pocket on the front of his pristine white polyurethane apron. Strips of seasoned biltong hung from large steel hooks in the wall. The butchery smelt of fresh meat and spice. Mr. Moyo's biltong came highly endorsed from far afield as the city. It was rumoured that he would soon open another butchery in the city.

On this particular Saturday morning my mother handed me the customary two dollar bill to buy our weekly allocation of meat, which I realised much later when I was older that it was not adequate to satisfy the needs in our home considering the number of people my mother fed daily but somehow she managed to miraculously make it stretch and the meat would last the week. With my friend Dora in tow

I made my way to the shopping complex. Walking up to the butchery we were chatting and laughing and then I caught a glimpse through the open doorway of a shelf in the convenience shop stacked high with clear containers full of mouth-watering candy. I had never seen so much candy in my life and awestruck I froze in my tracks with my mouth wide open. Seeing my amazement Dora followed my gaze and her eyes widened in wonder.

'So many sweets' she sighed with yearning.

I knew right then what I would do.

'I'll buy sweets with just some of the money then I'll buy meat with the rest of the money.'

Without a word we walked in and up to the counter and handed the crisp two dollar bill to the large lady standing behind the counter.

'Please may I have sweets?' I said mustering all the courage I could.

Her gaze swept over us curiously.

'You want sweets with **all** this money?'

'Not all of the money.' I replied quickly 'Just some of the money please.'

'Who gave you the money?' she queried, suddenly suspicious.

'My mother.' I responded truthfully with a wide eyed toothy smile.

She stood for what seemed an eternity quizzically looking at me holding out the two dollar bill in all earnestness and as if vacillating to the innocence in my big brown eyes she took the money. She tossed the money into a cash drawer and pulled out a dollar bill and a silver fifty cent coin which she dropped into my open palm.

'You got a shiny coin' Dora stated joyfully.

With that remark all trepidation at the decision I had made vanished.

'Look Shumi!' Dora exclaimed pointing. The lady behind the

counter smiled as she handed me a transparent bag full of the most delightful sweet treasures I had ever laid my eyes on. There were peppermint drops, flavoured jelly beans, sugary liquorice strips, rainbow coloured lollipops and sticky chocolate squares.

With the candy safely in hand we hurried next door to the butchery. Walking in, I noticed the shiny new machine on the steel counter top. I placed the dollar bill and fifty cent coin on the counter. Consternation flickered across Mr Moyo's face.

'What is that?' I quipped pointing at the machine on the counter, trying to avoid having to answer questions about what had happened to the customary two dollar purchase. 'That's a cash register' he explained with pride in his voice. 'It makes it easier to calculate every sale and to keep the money safe.' I noticed the wooden cash box with the big lock was no longer in its usual spot under the steel covered cabinet. Lifting chunks of fresh meat from the glass cabinets he placed the meat on a scale and packed the meat in brown paper wrapping. He placed the wrapped meat in the shopping basket. He walked over to the cash register and soon I heard bell like sounds coming from the machine. As a white paper strip with printed numbers rolled up from the inside of the machine he tore it off and carefully placed it in the shopping basket.

'Tell your mother in order for me to fulfil her weekly order she must maintain the $2 charge for the quota we agreed on.'

I nodded guiltily as he handed me the shopping basket. With a quick goodbye I hurried out of the butchery. As quickly as we could, Dora and I ran behind the shopping complex and sat down on a tree stump on the edge of a well beaten path that led to a dusty patch surrounded by leafy jacaranda trees which we called our playground. Several of our friends from school were already there lazily kicking a home-made plastic ball.

I waved the plastic bag with the candy excitedly as I called out 'Look!'

'Henry! Maggie! Verna! Come and get some sweets!' Dora yelled to the figures on the playground, beckoning them to come. Soon grubby hands appeared as they jostled in front of me. I generously handed out the candy amidst squeals of delight. We chomped, chewed and sucked as we worked our way through the candy bag. Soon all the sweets were finished and with a self-satisfied sigh, I waved goodbye to my friends and trekked back home with a bounce in my step. The home in which my mother now stood in the doorway to my bedroom ready to explode into a fit of rage holding the shopping basket.

'What...what is wrong mama?' I stuttered.

'*What is wrong*? **What is wrong?**' She exploded.

I shrunk back from the palpable anger in her voice.

'What is wrong is that I gave you $2 to buy meat but instead you return with $1.50 worth of meat! Where is the rest of the money?'

I shook my head in denial but my heart thundered in fear. How did she know? Who had told her?

'You'd better speak up Shumi or else!' The threat hung in the air. I swallowed back a sob as she threw a piece of white paper with printed numbers at me and it fluttered to the floor at my feet.

'Don't you lie to me either because that's the receipt right there!'

The receipt! Of course. The white strip of paper from the shiny new cash register was the source of my current discomfort. What was it that Mr Moyo had said? That it helped him calculate every sale. That was how my mother had discovered my dishonesty.

'I'm sorry mama!' I cried. 'I'm sorry!'

I knew what was coming next. She would get one of my father's belts and she would lay its thick leather surface across the back of my legs. She would give me five to six hard lashes and they would cut into my tender flesh, leaving angry welts that would gradually subside after a few hours. I could try to explain but would she understand. Would she understand that I had been compelled to buy the sweets? I had done it but at the core of my being I knew that what I had done was not for me. I did like candy and the candy was good to eat but more than that I liked how sharing the candy had made me feel. I liked to bring happiness as I remembered all the smiles and the unrestrained laughter on the playground. I had noticed the longing in the eyes of my friends when I opened my lunch box at school. Ordinarily packed with jam sandwiches, it was still more food than most of my friends carried to school. That is why I rarely ate the food that was packed in my lunch box preferring instead to give it to my friends with their silently pleading eyes. I was too young to understand what poverty was but my heart swelled with joy at the thought of giving-even if it was only a stick of candy. Would my mother understand how important it was for me to give my friends all I had because somehow I realised that they did not have as much as I was blessed to have – no matter how little that was by the world's standards.

'Mama please don't hit me!' I sobbed as she raised the black leather belt above her head and swiftly brought it down with a loud crack on my skin. Again and again. The cracking sound against my skin drowned by my woeful cries. My mother would never understand why I had bought the candy.

Later that evening as I lay in bed pretending to be asleep, next to my sister Rose my father returned from the tavern where he usually spent most of his days drinking. I did not run to greet him as I was accustomed to doing. After he ate my mother told him what had happened. There was no ceiling in our house and privacy was not completely possible because of the interconnecting gaps between the walls and the roof that ran from wall to wall, from room to room. They were in their bedroom speaking in hushed tones but their conversation floated over the timber trusses that criss-crossed under the roof.

'She has to go Baba.' My mom was saying with perceptible strain in her voice.

'She needs the discipline. I never experienced this kind of rebellious behaviour with Rose.'

'She's just a child Em.' He replied quietly. Em was my father's way of calling my mother which was a shortened version of her full name Emilia. It was a term of endearment that had started during courtship and had weathered the turbulence of their marriage; the vestige of a love that was no longer seen or felt.

'I know Baba but my hands are full right now at home with the baby. I just can't stretch myself any further to give her the full attention she needs. Especially now that I'm back at work full time. If only you...'her voice trailed off.

'If only I what Em?'

There was a strained silence.

'Say it! Spit it out! If only I could what? If only I could be a man and find a job right? Is that what this is about? You have an issue with me?'

'She's my child too Baba. She's my child but we are losing her if we don't do something radically different to discipline her. I hate to do this too but it's the only ....'

'So you have decided then!' He cut her off angrily. 'You are now the head of the house eh? You bring in the money and so you call the shots. What were you going to say? Finish your statement! If only I what?'

The bed creaked as my father stood up. An ominous silence settled in the house.

'No Baba! Please.' She pleaded.

The sudden crack of a belt in the silence jolted me into an upright position as my stomach churned and my mouth went dry.

'Baba, no! Baba!' she screamed.

I clenched my fists in blind anger and fear. The knot in my stomach tightened. My chest pounded. I could not breathe.

The whipping continued. My mother whimpered and the baby wailed.

Then just as quickly as it had started it suddenly ended. Something clattered on the floor. Their door was flung open and my father stepped out breathing heavily. I looked at our door. Would he come barging in and drag me out to beat me too? The sudden outbursts of violence were becoming more frequent. He had never raised his hand against me or my sister Rose and only my mother was the victim of his murderous rage but his dark moods had become unpredictable. I slid under the blanket as hot tears poured down my face. I loved my father dearly but I could see the monster he was becoming although I did not understand why. I missed my gentle attentive father. More tears spilled down my face and I suppressed the urge to scream. Then I heard the outside door slam shut as my father left in the night and a heavy silence filled the darkened house.

My mind was numb as I lay in the dark wondering if I should go to my mother. I was sorry for what I had done. I was sorry that my desire to share simple pleasures with my friends had fractured my family's happiness. I was sorry that the aftermath of an innocent morning spent sharing candy on a dusty playground was pain and devastation for the people I loved the most. I could feel Rose tense beside me. I knew she blamed me. Sometimes I thought she

'I LOVED MY FATHER DEARLY BUT I COULD SEE THE MONSTER HE WAS BECOMING ALTHOUGH I DID NOT UNDERSTAND WHY. I MISSED MY GENTLE ATTENTIVE FATHER.

hated me. I did not blame her. I was the cause of the tumult in our family.

I sobbed quietly as the baby wailed again.

'Stop your nonsense and go to sleep' Rose hissed harshly in the dark. 'This is all your fault!'

I pulled the blanket over my head on the wet pillow. Somewhere in the night the baby wailed, again.

# CHAPTER 3

In the ensuing weeks following that fateful night of violence I pretended that nothing had happened. I pretended that the violence had not ripped out my heart and in its wake left nothing but shards of fear. I smiled on the outside but on the inside I was a shell, devoid of all that was once hopeful and beautiful inside me. I understood what I felt but I was too afraid to put a name to what was happening to my parent's relationship. So I chose silence. If I did not lend my voice to the unspeakable pain, then I reasoned it would stop hurting so much. If I put all my effort in burying it deep down inside then perhaps the pain and fear, especially the fear, would be lost deep inside forever and it could never hurt me again. And so I did not speak. Not about the loneliness I felt surrounded by laughter and chatter in our home that somehow was no longer enough. I did not speak about how I did not recognise my father anymore and the pit in my stomach that churned every time he came home and how the laughter would die down and the chatter turn to whispers. I did not speak about the recurring dream I had; of a rolling cloud of darkness chasing me through our home as I screamed, running and falling in terror and I would wake up drenched in sweat and tears.

My mother did not speak too. She did not speak about the trauma of marrying the man she had fallen in love with and waking up next to a complete stranger. She did not speak about her daily fear of living in a home that could erupt in explosive violence at any sudden moment and maybe one day it would end her life. She did not speak about the humiliation and shame of raising three daughters, who would one day become women themselves in a home with a man who no longer loved her or cherished her. She did not speak about the sadness and isolation of what she saw as her private affliction, not until many years later. She too, like me, and many others in such circumstances chose silence.

Rose did not speak about it either although her angry eyes shot looks of blame at me each time my mother emerged from the bathroom with reddened eyes and a tear streaked face. She did not speak about the bruises on my mother's arms and back that sometimes we would glimpse when we walked in her room without warning while she dressed. Although her body would stiffen as she lay in bed next to me, my sister did not speak about the baby wailing in the next room while my mother cried softly as my father raged in the night. She did not speak about the heart wrenching mornings we would wake up to our mother's swollen lip or blackened eye. Rose took over a lot of responsibilities at home during that time. She was soon turning 17 and she would be off to college to study to be a teacher. She knew she was going to be away from home for months on end and it was as if she wanted to do all she could to make up for her pending departure. Or was it a desperate need to somehow show our mother that she cared because she feared that she would return from college one day and find everything had changed? That our mother would no longer be there? The thought haunted me constantly as it did my sister too I knew, but if we did not say it aloud then maybe it would not come to pass.

Silence became my comfort and my escape. Pushing away the pain into the recesses of my mind provided relief from the reality of the devastation which surrounded me. I could imagine I belonged in a happy family with a loving father and paint a different reality as long as I did not speak about my broken home and the trauma of my father's violence. But the silence also anchored the brokenness and pain in our family, reinforcing the isolation and absolving the brutality of my father's assault. Without our voices raised in dissent against his actions he was not restrained nor held accountable and the violence only escalated. I understand now that silence against a wrong is complicity and wilful participation in an injustice against the victim. Our conscience must awaken to the seductive salve of holding our peace when there is no peace offered to those who suffer as a result of our silence. Our voices must rise and never be silenced out of fear. This is how we serve humanity. But I was too young to save Mama from my father and so the beatings continued.

> 'I UNDERSTAND NOW THAT SILENCE AGAINST A WRONG IS COMPLICITY AND WILFUL PARTICIPATION IN AN INJUSTICE AGAINST THE VICTIM.'

My shopping responsibilities had been withdrawn. There were no Saturday trips to the butchery with Dora anymore. I could still go the playground to play with my friends but the laughter did not ring true anymore. I was still bubbly and I still shared the most hilarious stories but I was also quiet about what was happening at home and the silence was spreading everywhere. I felt the walls closing in on me and I needed to break out. I was 7 years old but I became an angry 7-year-old. Although studies reveal that children raised in abusive homes are more likely to be violent themselves in future relationships, I was not built for aggression with my small frame and typically sweet nature. The effects of the pain I was witnessing at home did not erupt in angry fights on a dusty playground. I knew that would only lead me to more trouble at home. I enjoyed learning and I was doing well in school. My teachers rewarded my academic efforts with approval and my peers applauded my success. I hid my pain well but the frustration and pain surfaced in a more insidious way. I began stealing.

I did not see it as stealing initially. I was getting back what I needed. The man I knew as my father had been replaced by a stranger, my own mother wanted me sent away and my sister barely spoke to me and when she did it was with barely concealed venom. I rationalised I no longer needed to seek their love or approval because I still had the love and approval of my friends. Not all was lost. And so began days that turned into weeks of furtively rummaging through my mother's purse when she came in from work and left it unattended on the kitchen table or in her bedroom when she was cooking with my sister or cousins in the kitchen. I did not take the notes in her wallet, instead limiting my ill-gotten weekly haul to the silver coins that she kept in a side pocket in her purse. Each purloined coin found its way to the convenience shop where my friends and I would buy a bag of an assortment of exquisitely delectable sweets and as had become our custom we would share the treat on the dusty playground behind the shopping complex.

I often wondered about where I would be sent. The most likely place was my grandparent's homestead in rural Masvingo. Uncle Francis had married and was no longer living with my grandparents. He had moved to Chiredzi, a small farming town east of Masvingo. We often visited my grandparents during Christmas holidays and I loved the freedom of running through the grassy plains and taking baths in the clear streams that flowed behind the homestead. Uncle Francis would visit too and I looked forward to his exciting stories about his adventures when he was still a boy. At the end of each day we would sit on a rocky outcrop just beyond the quiet stream and watch the sky burst into glorious golden-red hues as the evening sun dipped beneath the distant horizon. When the weather became hot and clammy in the evenings I would ask Gogo to sleep on the open veranda outside, under the stars, until the sky turned gold as dawn was breaking. It would not be so awful if I was sent to live with Gogo. She was gentle and loving and her soft hugs smelt of powder and soap. I also knew that she loved me, perhaps even more than my own mother did.

With each passing week I became more rash in my recklessness. I reasoned that since my mother would have me sent away at any moment I had to make the most out of the little time I had left. I found a semblance of misguided purpose in my misdeeds, a security I could not find in the instability of my home and the volatility of my father's dark moods. The fear of exposure did not diminish my continuing misdemeanour. My mother had noticed the pilferage. She had probed, questioned and demanded answers but nobody admitted any wrongdoing. There were too many people in the house to cast suspicion on any one individual and I kept my tracks well hidden. I did not carry the incriminating sweets back home. She had started locking the door to her bedroom when she was not at home but she often forgot to lock it when she was home and that was more time than I needed with her purse.

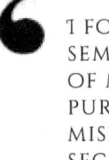

'I FOUND A SEMBLANCE OF MISGUIDED PURPOSE IN MY MISDEEDS, A SECURITY I COULD NOT FIND IN THE INSTABILITY OF MY HOME AND THE VOLATILITY OF MY FATHER'S DARK MOODS. .

In my naiveté I thought I would never be caught out and that was my undoing. I was soon to learn the truth of the adage, "pride comes before a fall." I remember the day everything unravelled. It was a Saturday morning and my mother had left for work earlier leaving my father asleep in their bedroom. I wanted to go candy shopping with my friends later that day but my mother had not left her purse within sight that entire week. I desperately needed money. So when providence smiled upon me half an hour later in the form of breakfast laid out on the living room table for my father I waited for him to sit down to his meal while he read the morning paper. When I was certain he was settled with a steaming cup of strong black tea engrossed in the paper I rushed in to my parents' bedroom.

Glancing furtively behind me to make sure nobody was coming in after me I quickly looked around for my father's jacket. It was hanging on the edge of the open closet door as though it had been carelessly tossed there when my father had come in late the previous night. As I hurriedly rummaged through the pockets searching for a silver coin my father walked in unexpectedly. I froze with my hand in one pocket as confusion swirled in my mind! He could not have finished his breakfast so quickly! He took in the scene with one look and as realisation of what I was doing dawned on him he lifted his gaze and for a moment it appeared as though he could see right through me. Then our eyes locked and I saw a look of such disappointment and desolation, it caught my breath. Suddenly I wanted him to punish me, to beat me with one of his belts, to lash out at me, to do anything but look at me with the haunting sadness I saw lurking in his eyes. I wanted the painful silence that stretched out interminably between us to end.

He picked up a belt which was hanging on a hook near the door and slowly he pulled the belt through the waistband of the khaki trousers he was wearing. All the while he was looking at me and his eyes glistened. A lump rose in my throat. He had walked into his bedroom to wear his belt when he had stumbled on his daughter stealing from him. I was too ashamed to look at him and so I looked away, feeling deeply humiliated. Would he hit me?

He broke the silence. 'Come and have tea with me.'

Numbly I dropped the jacket on the bed and followed him to the living room. He pulled out a chair as he headed into the kitchen returning with a cup and a bottle of milk. He poured tea into the cup and generously added milk.

'Two spoons of sugar?' he asked. I nodded silently.

'Do you remember when I took you and your sister to the Bernard Mizeki shrine in Marondera? You must have been about 5 years old. You asked so many questions I got tired I couldn't keep up and I ended up telling you that if you didn't stay quiet the spirits would be angry they would take you away.' He smiled. 'But then you asked if the spirits would answer your questions instead since they would have taken you' A wistful look came over his eyes. He looked at me. 'I just want you to know that you can ask me anything.'

He pointed at my untouched cup of tea. 'Drink up.'

I sipped the milky tea. He had made it just the way I liked it. I smiled. Slowly I regained my composure. After tea I cleared the table and he brought out his deck of cards. We spent the rest of the morning rehashing old stories and talking about all the things we had done together as we played card games. We laughed and chatted till it was midday.

After lunch he invited me for a walk to the shopping complex. When we walked past the convenience store he noticed my preoccupation with the candy display.

'You want some sweets Shumi?' he asked.

I stood still unsure how to respond. He walked in to the store and bought a bag of candy, just as I had done for so many weeks with Dora, only this time I was with my father. I led him to the playground behind the shopping complex and we sat on the tree stump and shared candy. I was giddy with joy at the thought that my father was finally emotionally available. The day was perfect and nothing would ruin it. We walked back home as the afternoon sun began dipping in the sky.

Later that evening as I was sitting at my father's feet in the living room my mother walked in from work. Surprise flickered on her face momentarily as she took in the cosy scene of father and daughter but she did not say anything as she put her bag down. My father stood up and stated simply, 'You were right Em. Shumi needs the discipline. Do what you need to do.' He patted my head, sighed heavily and walked out.

My heart sank. I was crushed. All day I thought my father and I had reconnected and that I was loved again. But I had been wrong! My transgression was too great to forgive. My father did not love me anymore just like my mother had stopped loving me all those years ago when she left me with Gogo. My mother turned to look at me with the same tormented look in her eyes I had seen earlier in my father's eyes.

'What happened Shumi? What did you do?'

'Nothing Mama.' Tears filled my eyes. 'Please Mama. I don't want to go.'

She knelt before me and in a rare display of affection she gently cupped my face in her hands.

'It's for your good Shumi. You will see. It won't be that bad.'

She wiped the tears trickling down my face with her fingers. She pulled me close and hugged me tightly. She smelt faintly of flowers and pine disinfectant. I sobbed into her bosom.

'I don't want to go Mama! Please don't make me.'

She squeezed tighter. 'Everything will be alright.' she whispered. I shuddered as my heart constricted in pain the sobs wracking my body. She held me tightly till my sobs ceased then she carried me to bed and sat with me till I fell asleep, broken and spent.

# CHAPTER 4

Three weeks later I discovered where I was to be *sent away*. It was a Saturday morning and Mama had gone to the city with my father. I knew she was not going to work that morning because she wore her favourite floral dress and the navy patent leather shoes with the bow that made her feet look pretty. When I asked where they were going she had just smiled mysteriously and waved goodbye as she left home. They returned several hours later, worn and sweating, carrying heavy packages that threatened to spill out of their arms. They set everything down in the living room with obvious relief. One item caught my attention; it was a huge black trunk case with my name emblazoned on the lid. I had seen those black cases before. One of our neighbour's sons had a case exactly like that with his name marked on the lid too. But he was much older than me and he attended school in another town, very far from home.

My mother pulled out a blue dress with a white Peter Pan collar and the same contrast on the sleeves.

'Here' she smiled. 'Try this on.'

Gingerly I lifted the dress inspecting it. 'Is this for me?'

'Yes it is.'

I skipped to my room happily, slipped into the dress that smelt very new and strutted out to the living room where my parents sat. Rose stood in the kitchen doorway, watching quietly.

'Look! It fits. I love it Mama! Thankyou Mama! Thankyou Baba!'

My father smiled approvingly as he handed me a wide brimmed blue hat with an emblem of flaming candles on either page of an open book and the words 'United we stand' embroidered on the front.

Revelation dawned on me. 'Is it a uniform?'

He nodded.

'I'm going to a new school?' Where?' I exclaimed in delight and amazement.

There was a slight hesitation before he responded. "Gokomere. In Masvingo.'

Surprise flashed in his eyes as I ran across the room , squealing with joy , leaping into his lap and buried my head in his chest.

'Oh Baba! Thankyou! I'm going to boarding school!'

'*Makorokoto* Shumi. (Congratulations Shumi).' Rose said quietly as she turned back into the kitchen.

I was going to boarding school. Reeling from the wonderful news I could hardly breathe with excitement. I was going away too just like the neighbour's son did every school term and when I returned I would have all the neighbourhood kids surround me just like they surrounded him, only this time it will be me telling them all about my exciting adventures in a boarding school far from home. The news was doubly exciting because I would be in boarding school in Masvingo close to my grandparents' home. And the significance of the opportunity was not lost on me; not only was I going to be the first in my family to attend boarding school but I would be attending the same school my mother had attended decades earlier, only she had attended it as a day scholar, in defiance of tradition that had sought to strip her of her independence and self-will.

I had heard the stories about boarding school. I was going to have my own bed! With my own linen! I would carry boxes of food and my family would visit me during the term with more food. I would even get pocket money! I laughed aloud. Going away to boarding school was a very good arrangement. I stopped mid celebration as it dawned on me that I would not be able to see my friends for an entire school term. I would not see my friend Dora. My heart ached as sadness tinged my joy. I was going to miss Dora with her gentle ways and big heart. I would make new friends though. It would be fun! I pushed the sadness aside. I would get enough pocket money to buy candy for Dora when the holidays came. It would be like old times again. Just two more months till the New Year and I would be off to school. I twirled in the living room. Mama was right, everything was going to be fine.

Dora cried when I broke the news to her. She sobbed inconsolably while I pled with her to stop crying. Soon I was crying too. Dora was my closest friend and the only person who truly understood me. She was like a sister. Rose was my sister and my blood but I struggled to relate to her and she barely concealed her impatience with me. Maybe it was the distance in the years that stretched out between us. Or maybe we were too different, raised in different eras. I had grown up in the dawn of national independence where freedom was a reality and new possibilities beckoned for the bold and so I was fearless while she had been born in the middle of a raging war and she knew the potency of fear more than the power of faith. Dora embraced life like I did and she found joy in questions, curiosity and wonder while Rose held on to the answers handed down by those who had asked the questions before her. Rose was family but Dora felt like a sister. My sister Tinashe was almost

'I HAD GROWN UP IN THE DAWN OF NATIONAL INDEPENDENCE WHERE FREEDOM WAS A REALITY AND NEW POSSIBILITIES BECKONED FOR THE BOLD AND SO 'I WAS FEARLESS WHILE SHE HAD BEEN BORN IN THE MIDDLE OF A RAGING WAR AND SHE KNEW THE POTENCY OF FEAR MORE THAN THE POWER OF FAITH.

a year old and she was starting to walk. She followed me everywhere and I liked being the source of her giggles and laughter but she was too young to be a real sister. Faced with the reality of what it meant to attend school in Masvingo, my mind balked at the thought of leaving Dora. How did I ever think it possible to live apart from the only sister I had? We sat on a tree stump on the edge of a dusty playground crying for more time that we both knew was running out.

The Christmas holidays came and went in a blur. We did not travel to Masvingo for the holiday festivities as we were accustomed to because Mama said that we would be back in Masvingo at the start of the school term when she would leave me at school. Baba killed a goat and we ate our fill. Dora had travelled to the countryside for the holidays so I spent most of the holiday indoors, assisting with the cooking and cleaning. I did not mind because I knew it would be a long time till I was back home again. 96 days to be exact! That seemed like an eternity to my young mind. Baba was less angry although he still spent most of his time away from home. The outbursts had stopped recently, almost completely. His last attack on Mama a month ago had been particularly vicious.

I vividly remember the screams that night as Mama begged for her life. I had crawled deeper under the blanket to shut out her mournful cries. After that night Tinashe was moved to sleep in our bed so that Mama could rest. Mama had stayed in her room for three days. She refused to eat and ordered that her door remain closed. Only Rose would go in daily with soapy water and a bucket to help her wash herself. I did not see the injuries she suffered but when she finally came out of her bedroom she was thin and frail, struggling to walk without assistance, a shell of her former self. I later overheard Rose tell my cousin Faith how Baba had kicked her repeatedly with booted feet while she lay helpless on the floor. I still loved my father but I knew I could never forgive the hurt he had brought into our lives. I hoped that going away to boarding school would dim the memories of the violence in our home. Perhaps one day I would completely forget. It was going to be good to leave home even though I felt at times that I was turning my back on my family.

But I was just a child. I could no longer carry the crushing burden of healing my broken family and yet I felt responsible for the rift that tore us apart. I blamed myself for my father's black moods and for my mother's coldness and what I perceived as indifference towards me. I looked like her with my pert nose, deep set eyes and ebony skin but I sounded like my father. She had said as much once when she was angry. It broke my heart to realise that I was like the man I knew she did not love. With that realisation I also knew that she could never love me. She was my mother but there was a part of her that rejected me and it wounded me deeply to feel unwanted and unloved by my own mother. I also blamed myself for the distance between Rose and me. She blamed me too and for once we both agreed on something. The burden of guilt was heavy on my shoulders and I embraced the welcome intermission presented in going away to boarding school for the school term even if it was just for three months at a time. I would make new friends and possibly find another sister who would become family like Dora had. The burden would ease once I was away from home. The unspoken indictments would end if only for a while.

Soon it was January the 10th and I stood outside our home. I was wearing my very new blue uniform and the wide brimmed hat covered half my face. I felt very important and quite grown up but I was also hiding a trace of sadness at having to leave all that was familiar. I bit my trembling lower lip. There would be no tears now. Not in front of everyone. My sister Rose and my cousins Faith and Precious were all standing outside the door leading back into the house. Several of my friends had also gathered at the gate to see me off. Dora was a forlorn figure standing off to the side visibly struggling with emotion. My heart sank. I waved at Rose and my cousins as they patted me on my back.

'Be good Shumi. Don't disappoint mom.' Rose whispered as she turned away.

My cousin Faith squeezed my hand encouragingly as I walked up to Dora.

'I'll be back soon Dora.' I said tentatively.

Dora's eyes welled up with tears.

'I'll bring lots of goodies for you.' I said choking back a sob.

Her eyes lit up as she smiled knowingly.

We had spoken about the food I would carry to school and even made lists of all that I would save to share with her when I returned. She brushed her tears away with the back of her hand and hugged me tightly. Maggie and Verna also came forward and soon we were hugging and laughing as we said goodbye.

'See you soon!' I waved back at all of them as Mama led me away to the bus station at the end of the street. My father was already ahead carrying my heavy black case and two other bags filled with food and school supplies. The bus would take us to the outskirts of the City where we would board one of several coaches that plied the long distance routes to surrounding towns. The City bus station was huge with endless bays with buses coming in every quarter hour to collect passengers. The station was teeming with people pushing and shoving for a place on the buses. It made me nervous to see so many people in one place but it was comforting to have my father close. He would protect Mama and me. He pushed his way towards a bus heading to Masvingo. The bus had just arrived in the bay and soon the doorway was blocked with heaving bodies. I saw his strong broad shoulders move steadily through the crowd and soon he was on the bus. He would secure places for us to sit once inside and wait for us to find our way onto the bus. After what seemed an eternity Mama and I finally embarked on the bus and we settled down for the long drive to Masvingo. The coach was filled with noise; from the local music blaring from overhead speakers, to the chatter of the people around me and the vendors hawking their wares loudly as they walked through the bus. I hardly heard anything. I was too excited. I was going to boarding school.

# HOPE

"THERE ARE FAR
BETTER THINGS
AHEAD THAN ANY
WE LEAVE BEHIND."

(C.S. LEWIS)

PART TWO

# CHAPTER 5

Gokomere Catholic Primary School was everything I had imagined it would be. It was much bigger than my school back home in Chitungwiza. But wait, that was no longer my school. This was my school now! I could say that with a sense of belonging. The place was steeped in history, from the stone church building with its ornate lancet windows running the length of the walls in homage to Roman architecture that had seeped into church designs centuries ago to the terraced outdoor amphitheatre with the same distinct stone masonry. The school was surrounded by well-maintained shrubbery and well swept grounds. The brick classrooms with polished brown earth floors and windows overlooking a view of rock outcroppings and densely packed indigenous mopane trees in the distance were the same classrooms my mother had walked into years before and it filled my heart with pride.

I felt a connection to this place more than I had felt I belonged at home. Despite the brave display of indifference that I showed to the lack of emotion I felt in my relationship with my mother, inside of me was a little girl longing to be loved by her mother and to finally receive her approval. It was only when I was older that I realised that it was this yearning which made me feel closer to Mama as I walked through the pathways of a school which she had once set foot on almost three decades earlier. This is where her mind had been inspired by her teachers as they opened her eyes and mind to new possibilities. I imagined the dreams she had nurtured as a young girl when she had sat in the classrooms listening to her teachers. I had dreams too. I would do many things but most importantly I would make Mama proud.

I was placed in the first class of the third grade and I settled into the daily routine of classes and studying interspersed with breaks for meals and sports. The learning process was both intense and fun. The teachers were attentive and receptive to questions from curious minds such as mine. I could ask as many questions as I wanted, as long as I made room to process the answers. My questions were welcome here! Excellence was firmly entrenched in the way of life and the high grades achieved by previous students were a starting reference point for the academic goals for current students. I made friends quickly and soon it felt like I had been there for years. I had a bed in a dormitory that housed 6 girls. I soon became firm friends with three of them, Judith, Elise and Tatenda. We would lay on our backs on a grassy patch beyond the sports field during lazy Saturday afternoons sharing stories about how we would grow up to be rich and successful and what we would do with all the wealth. The weeks flew by.

Saturday mornings were reserved for cleaning and washing. Periodically we would have dormitory inspections by the Matron MaHungwe, a stocky woman who always wore her hair covered in gaudy colourful head wraps. Her motherly look belied a will of steel and her even stricter disciplinary outlook on child care. She would watch over her wards like a hawk and she never missed anything. We often whispered that she must have magical powers that enabled her to know everything we did in her absence. Punishment for wrongdoing was meted out instantly. She carried a short rubber hose which she would use on the backs of any offenders' hands whenever she walked through the dining hall and dormitories which were the areas of her rigorous rule.

One Saturday each term was the designated parents visit day. The whole school looked forward to the visit. There would be an air of excitement pervading throughout the school on the morning of the Saturday visit. Students would wait expectantly near the school entrance watching the dirt road just beyond the gate for any sign of their family members and loved ones. I remember with fondness the first Saturday my family came to visit me. Mama wore her pretty floral dress and my father looked handsome in his sharply creased khaki trousers and crisp white striped shirt. I had never felt prouder! I hugged them tightly and after introducing them to all my friends I found a shady spot to sit under a tree and I could not stop talking for hours. They listened, enamoured with my tales of books, classes, my new friends and the ghastly food served in the dining hall. Soon it was time for them to leave and they left more food packages to take me through the weeks left ahead in the school term. With each passing term I became more interested in what was happening at home in my absence and rambled less about my school adventures. I was finally adjusting to life away from home and in an inexplicable twist I found that I missed being at home. Like a misplaced piece in a puzzle I had never felt that I belonged at home and yet now

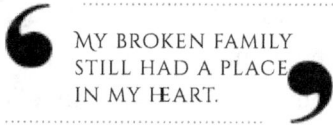

MY BROKEN FAMILY STILL HAD A PLACE IN MY HEART.

that I lived apart from my family I felt the void of the separation. My broken family still had a place in my heart.

Sunday mornings were dedicated to Mass, the weekly Sunday service run by the Catholic Church. A priest would be in attendance on Sunday mornings in his flowing robes and he would lead the service in a melancholic sing song voice that I hardly understood initially. Mass ran for 2 hours each morning and when the priest was not speaking it was filled with the sounds of soulful voices singing in unison which always stirred me to the core. There was something spiritual about the worship during Mass which I could not explain but it left me feeling hopeful; as though the ache in every painful experience in my life could be numbed even if the memory of it could never be erased.

I was too young to understand issues of spirituality but I believed I knew God. At the very least, having heard many stories about Him, I knew of Him. Our home was what I would call a Christian home in spite of the disparity of the dysfunction in which we lived. My father's violent behaviour came as no surprise because he did not practise the Christian faith. He was neither present at Sunday church services nor did he pray with us at home. Mama, my sisters Rose and Tinashe, my cousins and I attended morning service at the Methodist Church on the corner, two streets away from home. The pews were filled with mostly women and children with just a handful of men. The men all sat in one section of the moderately sized sanctuary while the women sat on the opposite end of the room. Children filled the middle section and teenagers and young adults occupied the back benches. I loved the singing. The room would reverberate with rapturous voices joined in harmony with the rhythmic drum. I always got goose bumps at the sound of the singing. This is what heaven must be like I often thought; filled with angelic voices in heartfelt praise. My mother had read a passage about how heaven was filled with celestial beings all proclaiming God's beauty and holiness. As the singing and the drums reached a crescendo I would feel an almost divine shift in the atmosphere as though we had opened a window into another realm; it was both reverential and beautiful.

Sunday service was an experience I looked forward to; the worship of a reigning deity who was both powerful and tender. The vastness of the world boggled my mind and yet God had created it all so that man could have dominion. That's what the scripture my teacher had read. That the world was created and humanity established to rule the world. My Sunday school teacher had said that we would all one day rule with God in heaven at the end of time. I imagined God exalted by powerful angelic beings serving at His feet while He was seated on a magnificent throne. I wondered if I would have a throne too. I had heard it said that God had hosts of angels at His command and in my mind's eye I saw thousands of angels flitting in and out of Heaven doing his bidding. I wondered about this great God Who had hands so big He could carry the whole world and I marvelled at how vast His power was to have created *everything* in the world only for Him to hand it over to humanity. It was too deep for my mind to fully comprehend but I was curious and wanted to learn more about religion and God.

I had overheard an argument between Rose and one of her high school friends. They had been studying outside on the veranda that afternoon and their books were laid out on the reed mat when the heated discussion began. They were disagreeing about the exact stages in the process of evolution in their debate on the theories of evolution. I could not understand the fundamental concepts of Darwinism theory they were passionately and loudly pointing out to each other nor did I grasp most of the complex references they bandied around effortlessly as they each made their point. I grappled to capture the essence of their academic debate; not only because of the big words they used which I could not pronounce but also because when I finally realised what they were in serious discussion about it I wondered why they would even question the origins of humanity.

Everybody knew that God had made the world and all that was in it. He had made a beautiful garden first and filled it with all that was lovely before God made the first man. Did Rose and her friend not know that already? My cousin Precious had read passages about the creation of the world from the Bible when I was younger before I could read. I liked that story best, a God who could magically create anything by just speaking. I could almost hear His voice which must have thundered in the empty void that was earth. I wished I had that kind of power, to speak life into existence. To create a new reality by just saying three words, 'Let there be...' Many years later in my adulthood I would come to realise the immeasurable creative power which lay in my own words. With the dramatic effect of the darkness that later filled my own life, I too became aware of the powerful life force of words. Simple unassuming words, words from a vocabulary I had used all my life. *"I can"* may very well have been the divine declaration *"Let there be!"* The limitless capacity of my imagination infused with the right words could build and establish my hopes or dreams or shatter them just as easily. The reality was that my response to the world I lived in; my choices, decisions and actions were shaped by my beliefs and my words. My only regret was If only I had known it sooner! I would have carried far less pain and more hope through the blistering adversity that lay ahead.

When I was able to read I had searched the bible for more stories, flipping through pages of God's consuming wrath that I barely understood and immersing myself in passages extolling the greatness and goodness of a merciful God. He was both love and judgement, peace and persecution, hope and despair. It all depended on where one stood in relation with Him. I wondered though where God had come from. I searched for the answers in sermons at church, both at home and at school. By this time at ten years of age I had made a decision to convert to Catholicism at school so I had begun attending catechism classes where the Catholic faith was explained and all the requirements laid out plainly for greater clarity. I searched for the origin of God in catechism classes but soon it became apparent that those kinds of questions were not welcome even in this liberal academic environment where curiosity was rewarded.

I asked my aunt Josephine this all important question once. She was my mother's cousin and she lived in Masvingo town, 12km away from school. There was a big Catholic Church in town but she preferred to attend Mass at Gokomere every Sunday and so she would drive out with her family every Sunday. After Mass while her two teenage sons chatted to the starry eyed girls from the high school, Aunt Jo and I would walk back to her car and she would give me bags of food for the week. It was too much food but I knew better than to protest because the food always found its way to a needy stomach particularly at a boarding school where I had observed that most students could not afford to bring food packages of their own from home. Unobtrusively, in my own quiet way I had found a way of extending the grace to others around me with these unexpected but welcome gifts from my aunt. I especially looked forward to the candy packs that she always made sure to include. We would sit in her car and talk about school and I would ask after my mother and Tinashe. I missed Mama and I worried about how she was coping without Rose who was now almost a qualified teacher in the city. So on this day my question caught her off guard.

'Aunt Jo where does God come from?'

She looked at me questioningly. 'Why would you ask such a question Shumi?'

'Why not Aunty? I know where I come from. I have a family. Who is God's family' I persisted.

'Jesus is God's family and the Holy Spirit too. And because of Jesus we too are now adopted into the family as sons and daughters. You know that already Shumi'. I detected exasperation in her voice.

'I know that Aunt Jo but who is God's father?' There. I had said it. The burning question was out in the open.

She glared at me angrily. 'Don't ask such silly questions Shumi!'

I was silent. She picked up her bag from the floor of the car and pulled out her car keys.

'I'll see you next Sunday Shumi. Hopefully this nonsense will be over by then.' She called to her sons and they drove away. I realised then that there were some things best left unasked but I still needed an answer one way or another.

My answer came sooner than I thought. There was a bookshop in the administration block at school that had a shelf solely set aside for a collection of books on the Christian faith. One book had stood out when I had ventured into the bookshop curiously seeking a book that would help me understand religion and faith. It was a book on prayer. I knew prayer was a very important practice in the Christian faith. Mama had once explained that prayer was communion with God and when I saw the green paperback with a cross on the cover and the title 'My little book of prayer', I was drawn to it. It contained a series of prayers on different issues that could be recited daily for a month. I began reciting the prayers quietly at bedtime just before the bell rang for lights to be switched off in the dormitories.

On this particular night I had hurriedly slipped under the covers on my bed to recite my prayers just before the lights went out. I pulled my book from beneath the pillow where I kept it for ready access and began reciting my daily devotion. As I finished the prayer and said 'Amen' the room fell into darkness as the lights were switched off. That's when I saw it. The cross on the cover of the book was glowing! I froze mesmerised by the sight of the glowing cross in the semi darkness. It was a soft iridescent light that spilled on my fingers as I touched the cross. I shut my eyes tightly and slowly opened them. I was not dreaming, the cross really was glowing! I called out to my friends in excitement in the darkened dormitory and they rushed to my bedside to see the phenomenon of the glowing cross.

'Look! The cross!' I cried half in fear and half in elation.

'What about the cross? Where is the cross?' Judith whispered in the dark.

'On the book! It's glowing! Can't you see?'

There was a stunned silence then voicing disbelief one of the girls said 'That's your torch glowing! There's no other reason why the cross would glow like that!'

'But I don't have a torch!' I protested as I waved my hands in the darkness.

'Stop lying Shumi!' one of the girls exclaimed. 'A book can't glow like that all by itself!'

Then another voice piped up 'The only glow you'll see is the flash of light from the blinding pain from MaHungwe's stick Shumi!' The room echoed with the guffaws of laughter from the girls.

'Shhh!' Judith whispered as they scurried back to their beds but it was too late. The room was flooded with light as the switch was flipped up. MaHungwe stood in the doorway and she was livid. After ascertaining the reason for the disturbance I received ten lashes for my part in the raucous disturbance. I did not tell MaHungwe about the glowing cross. I was in enough trouble already.

Years later as I reflected on the incident of the glowing cross I thought about humanity's resistance to believe. It is far easier to resist than to admit that it is possible because then the burden of changing and directing our actions in alignment with our beliefs becomes too great to bear. Especially in matters of faith and in the things of God where human intellect fails to contain the supernatural expanse of God. Controversy and polarisation to this day exists in what constitutes our beliefs. In the grand scheme of creation God has made room for humanity to reign in life. That our lives often do not reflect this authority is not because it is a fallacy as some would claim but it is ignorance on our part. However, ignorance does not change the truth.

Placed at our disposal is the capacity to lead successful lives and triumph in every arena of our lives even in the face of insurmountable odds but that capacity lies dormant for the majority resulting in unfulfilled lives still struggling with limitations and lack because our beliefs and thoughts are not aligned to who we are meant to be. Our fear of the possibilities and the miracles waiting in the wings clouds our willingness to take the risk of believing. More ashamed of believing and then trying only to fail the majority would rather stay stuck in stagnant places while our lives bleed dry. That is why it is easier to be blind to the glowing cross experiences in our lives. Our fear makes it easier to miss the unmistakable miracle and dismiss it for a trick on the senses. Yet God does not need to meet us at our point of reference, at our level of limited knowledge. God points to a higher way, a standard grander than we could ever imagine and it fills us with dread to see how high we ought to reach. In order to access the truth of our power in a deficient and failing world we have to meet Him at the higher plane of embracing His abundant promise in the purpose and truth of who He has created us to be. We can no longer afford to deny the greatness that is in us.

As the room settled into a cacophony of soft snoring and gentle breathing I was still wide awake. I understood now what Mama meant when she had said prayer was communion with God. It was not a one-way dialogue either. God could talk back to me too. He had just spoken to me through the glowing cross. Somehow I knew that it was why only I had seen the cross and nobody else could understand. Suddenly it occurred to me that it did not matter where God had come from or who His family was. I was asking the wrong question. God was before time itself and throughout time humanity would experience the divinity of His presence through purpose and will. When our souls were restless He was present as the peace we felt when we sought the answers to our quest. His flawless plan to restore and reconcile us to a destiny far greater than we imagined was centred on the faith response of humanity. The question to ask instead was why God cared deeply for humanity. My mind balked at the idea of a God who loved me more when I did not know of Him or love Him yet. As I drifted into sleep I whispered "I believe even if nobody else does."

> THE QUESTION TO ASK INSTEAD WAS WHY GOD CARED DEEPLY FOR HUMANITY. MY MIND BALKED AT THE IDEA OF A GOD WHO LOVED ME MORE WHEN I DID NOT KNOW OF HIM OR LOVE HIM YET.

# CHAPTER 6

I t was 1987 and while the world watched with bated breath as the President of the United States, Ronald Reagan met with the Russian premier, Mikhail Gorbachev at the Washington Summit for a historic meeting during which both countries signed an arms control treaty marking the beginning of the end of the Cold War, closer to home I celebrated a momentous occasion in the life of my hero, Moses Chunga. I had been introduced to soccer by my Uncle Francis and I soon became an avid fan of his favourite team, Dynamos Football Club or De-Mbare as it was affectionately called, a top tier club based in one of the populous high density suburbs of Harare. Moses 'Razorman 'Chunga was a talented midfielder who went on to become Zimbabwe's greatest midfielders. Moses Chunga had joined the Warriors, the Zimbabwe National Football Team, and they led a successful campaign in the 14th edition of the CECAFA Cup tournament placing second after Ethiopia. I was elated at the achievement. In the same year my father viciously attacked my mother for the last time.

My life plunged into free fall. I was 10 years old and for as long as I could remember growing up I had witnessed first-hand the brutal violence unleashed upon Mama by my father. Her body bore the evidence of the physical trauma she endured at his hands; a swelling lump on her forehead, a blackened eye, a bloody nose, a bruised lip. What unseen horrors lay hidden beneath her clothes? The harrowing effects of the turmoil she suffered went beyond the physical. She lost her way, submerged in a sea of pain that was suffocating the life out of her. She did not laugh anymore and her movements were not as fluid or graceful as I had remembered. Instead her movements had become slower and more mechanical as though she was struggling to function, her days blanketed in a vice like stupor and pain filled daze from which she could not awaken. I knew Mama's plight was not a unique one. I had heard the stories whispered in hushed conversations. I too had friends who quietly suffered the tragic pain of violence in the home. There was nothing else to be done about this terror that tore at the heart of a community, ripping families apart while the world watched in horrified silence. It was that complicit silence that hurt more than the tragedy unfolding in terror filled homes.

IT WAS THAT COMPLICIT SILENCE THAT HURT MORE THAN THE TRAGEDY UNFOLDING IN TERROR FILLED HOMES.

The effects of the violence were visible in our home. Each school holiday however I experienced anew a terrifying level of paralysing fear whenever my father's unpredictable moods turned into physical violence. The ferocity of each attack escalating with each outburst. I dreaded going home at the end of the school term afraid to watch my mother's brokenness fracture deeper each passing day. Rose was now a qualified teacher in the citrus farming town of Mazowe, south of Harare and she no longer lived at home. She would visit every holiday for a month and return to school at the beginning of the school term. She had taken up the role of running the household when she would visit, filling in where my mother no longer had the strength to carry on. I had been at boarding school for three years now so I did not encounter my father's violence as often as my 4-year-old sister Tinashe did. Tinashe was a sensitive child who was sickly with chronic health issues conceivably caused by the crisis at home. She frequently had episodes of respiratory distress during which her constricted breathing would leave her frail body wracked with pain as she struggled to breathe. The doctor in the city had diagnosed asthma and she was on medication to help her manage the symptoms of each asthmatic attack. The doctor had also suggested that the origin of her affliction was possibly psychosomatic.

I had loved my father as deeply as I now hated him. I had known a man who was gentle as he was intelligent, a man whose brilliant mind had steered mine to always seek out truth and knowledge but that man was buried deep inside the savagery of another who emerged to take his place. The monster resurfaced a week before I was to return to school. It was the last week of the winter holiday. The short, cold winter days had given way to longer, sunnier days as winter prepared to depart with her ice cold robes that had cloaked the country for almost four months. The sun was descending in the west casting its red glow on my skin as I sat on the veranda in the fading light. I was sitting with my cousins, Faith and Precious, who were now fully grown women. Faith was betrothed and was soon to be married in the coming month while Precious was in her second and final year of studies at a secretarial college in the City.

Precious was teasing Faith about her questionable cooking skills and had remarked that the dowry next month should be set aside because Faith's husband to be was undoubtedly going to demand it back after tasting her cooking. We were laughing amidst Faith's loud protests when a shadow fell across the path leading to the house. My father had returned several hours earlier than we usually expected him back. With a cursory glance in our direction he lumbered into the house, slamming the door loudly behind him. Mama was in the house.

She had returned from work earlier that afternoon. I had seen her moments earlier in the kitchen with Rose as they made preparations for supper. My heart thudded in my chest. I stood up and walked to the gate. I would go to visit Dora I decided. I stopped and looked up at the darkening sky. The sun was already disappearing over the horizon and soon it would be completely dark. It was too late to visit. I stood for a moment, rooted to the ground. Slowly I turned and retraced my steps back to where my cousins sat, passing them quietly as I opened the door.

'Am I not to eat in this house?' my father barked loudly. He was standing in the living room, breathing heavily, his features contorted in rage. I could see my mother trembling in the kitchen as tears filled my eyes. Rose walked out with a covered plate of food on a tray and silently, she set it on the small wooden table in the living room and walked back to the kitchen. He glowered at her retreating back and ferociously kicked the table. The plate toppled to the floor with a loud crash as food spilled out, leaving a trail of oily gravy on the walls. A deathly silence permeated the room.

'So my wife is too educated to serve her husband! I have to receive my meals from children!' he thundered. His bloodshot eyes glinted wildly in the waning light.

'Did I not marry? Did I not pay the customary cows for the bride price? Shall I be disrespected in my own home just because my wife has a job and I do not!' he snarled.

My mother walked out of the kitchen, her pinched features painfully drawn. I had not realised how thin she had become. She was wasting away right before my eyes and I had not noticed it before. A lump rose in my throat as the tears trickled down my face.

'I'm sorry Baba.' My mother stood quivering before him, her gaze lowered.

His hand struck out and caught her on the cheek as he punched her. She staggered backwards her head hitting against the leg of the upturned table as she crumpled to the floor. She moaned softly, her body curled up in a ball on the floor. He dropped to one knee pulling her up to a sitting position and viciously punched her again. His clenched fists pummelled her flailing body, again and again. Her hands fluttered upwards to his face in a feeble attempt to stave off more blows.

'You dare fight me woman! You fight me?!' he screeched hysterically. His eyes glazed over as his hands closed around her neck, stifling the life out of her. She writhed weakly under his vicious grip, making deathly gurgling sounds. My mother was dying and I was helpless to save her from the man I called father. Anger, blinding terror and pain came rushing up as I shuddered in fear.

'Baba please! Please stop! You're killing her!' I screamed as I ran across the room.

His rage fuelled eyes flickered upwards as he looked at me and suddenly his fingers on her neck slackened. He looked down at my mother's prone figure on the floor as he slid down and sat on the floor.

'Is she alive?' his voice thick with emotion. Was it fear? Shame? Or regret? I could not move. My mother stirred on the floor as tears of relief and helplessness splashed down my face. With the help of my cousins who had also witnessed the savage attack, Rose carried our mother to her bedroom. I picked up Tinashe who was crying softly in the kitchen. My father continued to sit on the floor surrounded by broken shards of the porcelain plates.

The following morning, I woke up to find my mother and Tinashe gone. Rose later tersely informed me that Mama had left for my grandparents' home in Masvingo. She had been unresponsive when I had asked when Mama would return. A week later I travelled back to school accompanied by Rose who, after leaving me at school, made her way back to her teaching job in Mazowe. I later discovered that Mama stayed in Masvingo for two months on official emergency leave from work. During those two months in Masvingo she applied for a lateral transfer from her nursing position at the hospital in Harare to Gweru, a town in the cooler low-lying midlands of Zimbabwe. After finding a nurse based in Gweru willing to transfer to Harare my mother had rented a house in the densely populated suburb of Mkoba in Gweru and started her new life as a single parent and working mother.

A delegation from Masvingo comprising Mama's uncles and her brother Uncle Francis had visited my father in the aftermath of the attack. Their demands were precise and unyielding; dissolution of their marriage on the grounds of his attempt to kill her. Brian and Emilia Kawa were customarily divorced after twenty years of marriage. Upon conclusion of their deliberations they collected all of my mother's belongings. The relationship between my parents had irreparably broken down many years earlier but sometimes the stark reality of desperate circumstances takes a moment to catch up with the inevitability of the truth. It is difficult to walk away from familiar places even when we are hurting in those toxic places. But the longer we stay in a state of denial the greater the cost of our freedom. Mama paid dearly for sustaining the dying embers of her marriage until the day her husband almost killed her. Like the thunder heralding the storm the violence erupted with such brutality that the truth could no longer be denied. In one afternoon, just as suddenly as it had started it finally ended, my parent's marriage was formally dissolved and all our lives were changed irrevocably. Precious and Faith moved out by the time the delegation arrived home. My unemployed father now alone without his wife and his family and without the means to fend for himself materially left for his parents' homestead in Marondera, leaving tenants in what was once our home.

# CHAPTER 7

A new era in history dawned in 1988 as the Soviet Union began its gradual dissolution into 15 independent republics. In the same year my soccer icon Moses Chunga made history when he became the first Zimbabwean footballer to move to a European club, Belgian side Eendrach Aalst Football Club, much to my unrestrained delight and excitement. His notable accomplishment in scaling the heights of international stardom for a young man I had heard Uncle Francis recount had been raised in very humble surroundings fuelled my own dreams of finding greatness in my own life. He became a reminder that greatness was possible. As a young black girl with audacious dreams I embraced the possibility of finding my own place in history. I did not have to wait long. In 1988 I was part of a historic moment in my country. I received and welcomed a world leader.

Pope John Paul II was the respected head of the Roman Catholic Church and the sovereign of the State of the Vatican City. Officially resident in the Apostolic Palace of the Vatican City his pontificate began in 1978. He was a well-travelled church leader globally, bearing a message of hope and unity, and ten years into his papacy he visited Zimbabwe. Post-independence Zimbabwe had witnessed years of tribal violence. Eight years after the country had won its right to sovereignty the war still raged on within its borders, only this time the battle lines were clearly drawn, brother against brother. The Pope's visit on the wings of a message of peace and reconciliation was predicted to be a timely salve to a brutalised nation.

His greatly anticipated visit on September 12 1988 had been meticulously planned by the Roman Catholic Church leadership in Zimbabwe. Tens of thousands of faithful believers were expected to attend the biggest Mass in the history of my country. Altar servers, ushers, choristers and other officials to assist with the administration of the event were carefully handpicked by a specially convened committee. My aunt Jo had risen through the ranks of the Catholic Church in the Gweru Diocese, a regional branch of the Church. A big hearted and philanthropic woman she contributed generously and frequently to the Church, and so when she suggested her niece was available to welcome the Pope with a garland of flowers as scheduled in the official reception plan, the idea was warmly received by the committee.

I stood in front of the mirror and twirled in delight. Aunt Jo had bought a shimmery white taffeta and satin dress with a bead encrusted bodice adorned with a bow on the waistband. The full skirt flounced softly around my legs as I admired my reflection in the mirror. My white shoes gleamed in the morning sunlight streaming through the open window. I quivered with anxiety and anticipation at the enormity of the occasion ahead. Giddy with joy and excitement I smiled. I was going to meet the Pope in person. The reception was to be conducted just before Mass was to be held in Bulawayo at a race track. The venue had been chosen for its capacity to host a massive gathering of devout Catholics who would travel from as far afield as South Africa and Botswana. It was a momentous occasion in the country's history now held together by a fragile peace accord signed into existence by the main warring factions only a year ago. I was not only going to witness this historic event but I was going to be part of it too.

Aunt Jo's voice broke into my reverie as she called out to tell me the garland of flowers had arrived. It was time to leave for the official reception. I sat in the car with Aunt Jo as she drove southwards out of the city. The race track was located on a stretch of land a short distance from a glistening franchise hotel. The road became densely packed with slow moving traffic as we neared the turn to the race track. Through the window I could see the swelling numbers of people making their way to the entrance of a heavily guarded metal gate. My aunt drove carefully threw the great multitude of people milling outside waiting their turn to be admitted. She slowed down to a complete standstill at the gate as a police officer peered into the car requesting to see documentation. She produced a letter with an official stamp from her bag and after a perfunctory look at the laminated paper he waved us through. There was a throng of more people inside the race track. Yellow and white Vatican flags fluttered in the air as exuberant voices were raised in unison in song. The sound of their worship gave me goose bumps.

An elevated podium had been erected in the centre of the track. A white tent covered the seating area. Priests in flowing black cassocks sat in the seating area. The silk scarlet brocade on the cassocks of the Bishops as well as their scarlet lined headdress denoted the hier- archy of the assemblage. An air of expectancy hung in the air. An altar covered in fine white linens with a golden chalice in the centre took centre stage. A carpet ran from the podium down a short flight of stairs to a receiving stand where I now stood. This is what history looks like I thought proudly. A cheer rippled through the crowd as the vehicle carrying the Pope came into view. A lump rose in my throat. The Pope was standing in the open vehicle waving serenely to the jubilant crowd. Thunderous applause filled the race track. My heart hammered in my chest as fear gripped me momentarily. Would I remember what I was to do? What if I stumbled and fell in front of all these people? My hands grew clammy as I held onto the garland tightly. Panic surged through my body, I was crushing the flowers! I loosened my grip and breathed deeply. The vehicle drew nearer.

The pope was a diminutive man with gentle intelligent eyes and a kind smile. He wore a regal *ferraiolo*, a cape, over a spotless white ankle length cassock. His jewelled white silk high headdress with ornate stones surrounding an embroidered gold cross glinted in the sun. I remembered the glowing cross several years ago in a darkened dormitory on the cover of my book of prayers. I smiled. Divine providence had guided me to this very moment! I curtsied as I presented the garland of flowers to him and relieved that I had done is seamlessly without any embarrassing incident I flashed a happy smile. He held my hands briefly and the thought of how I would never wash my hands ever again briefly flitted through my mind. As the crowd continued cheering wildly, we walked up the steps leading to the podium. At the top of the stairs as he moved away to the altar and I was led to the seating area, he slipped something into my hand. I looked down at my open palm and smiled. How did he know I wondered in amazement at his retreating back? A tin foil wrapped sweet lay in my hand.

At the end of Mass celebration, we left for a huge luncheon at the hotel we had passed earlier in the morning. The rest of the day passed in a blur of activity of posing for photographs, polite smiling and hand shaking with various delegations. I was thankful to head back home by the time the shadows lengthened and evening fell. I had met the Pope that day and I cherished how special and unforgettable the memories I had made that day would be carried in my heart always. Later that night I reflected on what I wanted to accomplish with my life. When you are young it all seems possible. It was easier to dream when I was not crushed under the weight of life and a cascade of negativity that seemed to follow me as I grew older. I wanted to be a leader. As I lay in bed my thoughts wandered to the kind of leader I wanted to be. I wanted the world to love me just like the crowds had cheered jubilantly at the sight of the Pope. I wondered how I would respond to that kind of love and admiration. Being loved was vitally important to and I wanted to be the kind of the kind of leader who would love humanity and make a positive difference in the world just like the Pope. His message of love and peace was stirring up unity in a fractured world. I wanted to do something as deeply profound with my life.

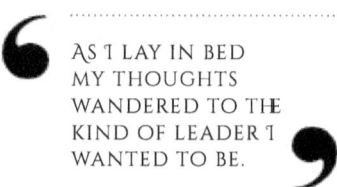

AS I LAY IN BED MY THOUGHTS WANDERED TO THE KIND OF LEADER I WANTED TO BE.

I was fascinated by the power he wielded in his position as a religious leader. He was a man of faith and yet he was a recognised world leader. It was that position which allowed him to have a huge impact globally and yet purpose is what had paved the way for his sovereign position. I wondered where my purpose would lead me. I knew what my purpose was, that I was destined to serve. I just did not know how I would come to be influential in my purpose. I understood that the Pope's influence meant greater visibility and access to the world. As I pondered on the role in my life which I could pursue so I could do more and serve without restraint it suddenly occurred to me how I could do that. I would become a nun! After meeting the Pope, I knew then just how important my faith was to me. My purpose would be to live a life unencumbered by worldly standards while my faith deepened and God would find a big place in the world for me to serve Him. My heart filled with such a warm feeling that I smiled as I hugged the blankets closer. I would tell Aunt Jo in the morning.

# CHAPTER 8

The last two years of primary school sped by swiftly. Since Mama had moved to Gweru, I now lived in Gweru over the school holidays. Living in Gweru meant a shorter travelling distance back to school each term but it also meant that I could no longer be with my friends in Chitungwiza. I missed Dora especially. Life in Gweru was much quieter than I was accustomed to growing up. My cousins, Faith and Precious no longer lived with us and fewer relatives visited. My mother lived with Tinashe, who was now enrolled at a local primary school a short walk from home, while I was away at school. Tinashe's health improved dramatically in the first year of relocating to Gweru. Her asthma attacks vanished almost completely and the timid, sickly child blossomed into a well-adjusted albeit shy girl who loved to spend hours quietly playing with her collection of dolls. Rose was married in my senior year at school and only came to visit twice a year, during Easter and Christmas holidays.

While our lives settled into a semblance of normalcy my mother's struggle to adjust to her new life was painful to watch. The strong willed village girl who had triumphantly fulfilled her dreams of independence and self-directed success was now a survivor of domestic violence, desperately fashioning a new life for herself in a new town where she was careful to hide the circumstances of her past. She did not speak of her past trauma but I saw the pain registered in her eyes each time she evaded questions about her marital status from inquisitive neighbours. And so the isolation continued. First it was the stigma of being a victim of abuse in a loveless marriage that had confined her to a lonely life for most of the later years of marriage to my father. Now it was the social blemish of being labelled a divorcee that caused her to retreat deeper into her shell. I wondered why women shunned my mother. I wondered why they pointed furtively in her direction when her back was turned and they thought she could not see them. But I could see them and I wondered why they whispered when she approached, falling silent as she walked past. She found it difficult to make friends with most married women with families in the neighbourhood. In hindsight I realise that, they were either too unyielding, too uncompromising to understand her pain or perhaps they were too insecure to relate to an attractive, working, single woman in her early forties raising children without any help.

In later years in my adulthood I read a damning report by Professor Mary Osirim on the scale of violence against women in Zimbabwe. Her study was based on data collected between 1988 and 1990 and the report grimly estimated that women were beaten by their partners in six out of ten homes. That 60% of women suffered violence at the hands of an intimate partner was reprehensible and that the violence continued to exact its emotional toll on the survivor long after the abuse ended was unimaginable. Self-inflicted, self-sabotaging traits would remain evident as did other forms of behavioural dysfunction which I saw in Mama. What she needed most was social support and supportive therapy in her journey to healing in the aftermath of the horror of violence at the hands of her husband and yet she feared the judgement that she knew would come if people knew and so she kept her painful secret well hidden. I realised much later that Mama's instinct to withdraw from the world was not just her way of securing her painful past from exposure but it was also a symptom of something much deeper and more sinister; her loss of self-esteem. Tradition and archaic social norms and customs had failed to shake her infallible belief in herself at a younger age, she knew that she was not only competent to direct her life towards lofty goals but that she was also worthy of the recognition and rewards of her effort. Sadly, society's judgemental silence after her brutalisation had now succeeded in shaming her simply because her marriage had failed. That womanhood and pain were somehow inextricably intertwined was unmistakably evident. It did not matter what a great success a woman was if she could not stay married, even if the cost of sustaining that status meant losing her own life. If her marriage failed, then she had failed. Perceptions in society placed less value on a woman with a failed marriage despite the roaring success apparent in other aspects of her life My mother knew all too well the shame. That she had overcome great difficulties in her life and was alive to tell the tale, a tale of surviving harrowing violence in her home, somehow that was of less significance.

> PERCEPTIONS IN SOCIETY PLACED LESS VALUE ON A WOMAN WITH A FAILED MARRIAGE DESPITE THE ROARING SUCCESS APPARENT IN OTHER ASPECTS OF HER LIFE MY MOTHER KNEW ALL TOO WELL THE SHAME.

At the start of each school term I had found it increasingly difficult to leave my mother for boarding school. As the time for high school applications advanced I had to make a decision about whether I would continue at Gokomere or I would move to a school closer to home. I was filled with an irrational fear that if I left home something terrible would happen to my mother. Despite the fractures in our relationship in the early years of my childhood I cared for her deeply. I realised that in some way the wounds I was struggling with stemmed from feelings of abandonment I felt when she had left me to return to work and I was raised by Gogo. Resentful that she had picked my sister Rose over me I had only begun to understand why she had made that decision when I saw the difficulties she faced in raising Tinashe on her own. As a very young child I would have required more time and attention in care giving than my older sibling. I could not easily mend the relationship with Rose who was no longer living at home with us as she had her own family but I could certainly try to show Mama that I loved her.

Towards the end of my primary school year I decided to apply to attend a school closer to home for high school. I wanted to live closer to Mama. Secretly I hoped that it would restore the bond between mother and daughter which I yearned for. Mama would not hear of it. She threatened and screamed and finally resorted to weeping and begging when I resolutely resisted her attempts to change my mind. I reasoned that she would eventually see the sense in my decision in the not so distant future. I would not leave her, not until she no longer winced from the pain of her past at the mention of my father's name. Her life still bore the effects of the loneliness and pain wrought by her union to a man whose very memory continued to plunder life and hope from her even after he was no longer in her life.

I thought of my father often after my parents separated and I would wonder how he was living without us. He did not visit and neither did he write or call. As time passed I had to remind myself that I still had a living father. I did miss him sometimes. Perhaps I thought I thought I did or at the very least I simply missed having a father to talk about. My friends would speak of their fathers and I ached deeply for my own father. The father I had loved before he unravelled into psychotic rage and fury. Initially after my parent's separation I had travelled to Marondera to visit my father. Over the holiday, Aunt Jo would take me to Harare on one of her frequent business trips and on each

trip she would make the time for an afternoon visit with my father in
Marondera which was an hour's drive from Harare. Lately the visits
had stopped. My father had fallen ill. How unwell I later discovered
when I overheard a conversation between my mother and Aunt Jo. He
was suffering from severe depression. His condition had been exacer-
bated by the loss of his job and subsequently the loss of his confidence
in his identity as a providing father and husband. It was the feeling
of disempowerment that had proven too much for his already fragile
mind to bear causing him to erupt into manic violence and in a tragic
twist it was that violence that ultimately cost him the family that he
desperately needed in order to heal. Alone, he had finally caved under
the strain of his grief and his world became a silent, dark place. I had
gone to my room and wept for my father. I knew I did not love him the
way I had loved him before he became a monster but I wept for what
could have been.

If Mama had known what was wrong with him earlier in their
marriage when he retreated only to emerge in violent outbursts would
my father have been saved? Maybe he would have sought help professionally and our lives would not have been shattered. However, I
knew the truth. At that young age I did not understand the magnitude
of my father's diagnosis. I only felt the shame and even though I did
not speak of it I felt tainted by it. My professionally trained mother, a
seasoned nurse practitioner herself, would not openly speak about the
psychological affliction my father was struggling with. Like a shameful
secret his mental health crisis became an unspeakable disease which
could haunt the family and destroy our future. His struggle had to be
carefully hidden from a judgemental society. If it were to be revealed
that my father's inability to cope with life after returning home from
years in a bruising war only to lose his job had caused him to descend

into manic depression and loneliness would only serve to attract more whispers and pointing fingers in our direction.

Many years later when I was now an adult I pondered at the absurdity of a society which demanded the appearance of wellbeing based on material wealth and economic success from a broken man regardless of the validity of his struggles with his circumstances. His downward spiral into the darkness of his mental anguish had been fuelled by the perception of what he concluded was his meaningless existence in a fast evolving world. This realisation had probably driven him into a state of despondency and eventually led to emotional detachment from his family. The deafening silence around mental health

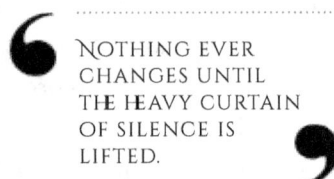

NOTHING EVER CHANGES UNTIL THE HEAVY CURTAIN OF SILENCE IS LIFTED.

issues contributed to the breakdown my father suffered. The stigma of his mental health condition shuttered awareness and I lived in fear of the curse of his struggles in my own life. After all Mama had said I was more like him. How would I escape the stain of his sickness? I had nobody to ask and so I kept silent, my mind in anguish. Nothing ever changes until the heavy curtain of silence is lifted. Silence became an ally of ignorance in a war of shaming a family in crisis. A war we lost once the whispering and finger pointing started, untruths floating in shameless gossip. Many years later secrecy still shrouds the suffering of individuals and families struggling with mental illness. Much has to change in our communities.

# CHAPTER 9

I won the stand-off. Regina Mundi, a school for girls which was located on the outskirts of Gweru, became my new home in high school. The school also offered boarding facilities for students. I was adamant to not leave Mama so I opted to attend day school at the Catholic girls' high school which was run by the Sisters of the Jesuit Order. I was doubly happy because my friend Judith had also transferred to the same school although she was a boarding student at the school. Every morning on weekdays I would depart for the school bus which picked up attending day students from various pick up points at 6am and spend the day in classes at school. At the end of the day, tired and weary from a full day of learning and an afternoon of sporting activities, I would make my way home just before sundown. I relished the quiet evenings with Tinashe and my mother as we ate supper, finished off homework and then nodded off to sleep feeling whole and happy. It was more than I had hoped for. I no longer had to worry about Mama and Tinashe was glad to have her sister living at home. Mama was safe and I was happy to be home.

Towards the end of my first year in high school my mother petitioned the head Sister at the school, Sister Monica at the time, for my transfer from attending day school to a full boarding student. Initially I was reluctant to make this move but after an eye opening talk with Sister Monica I became aware of a fact I had not fully considered. She observed that perhaps I had taken the role of being my mother's protector because I had not brought the issue before God in prayer. If I had prayed about my concerns for my mother, then perhaps I did not trust God to protect her sufficiently. She went on to remark that even though I had taken this grave responsibility I was failing dismally in discharging my duties competently because of one singular limitation; my inability to be everywhere at once and to know everything that was happening. How could I possibly know all the injustices my mother faced at home, at work, at church, when I was not there? But God was omnipotent, she pointed out. He was all-seeing and therefore only He could minister the healing my mother needed just at the right time she needed it. In the end I conceded to Sister Monica's wisdom. She was right, leaving home would allow me to release the irrational fear that constantly plagued me that something would happen to Mama. I too was in need of healing from the trauma of growing up in a violent home but by holding on to the fear of a terrible tragedy to befall my mother I was holding on to the trauma of the past violence of my early childhood. I needed to let it go. More importantly it would also be an act of great faith to entrust God with what was most precious to me-my mother, and I needed to remember that I was a child of faith.

The high school years were the best years of my life. Teenagers throughout time are on one hand either sure about themselves, or at the very least confident in their abilities to achieve great success, perhaps cocky even or on the hand they are plagued by raging insecurities in themselves in many aspects ranging from body image issues to academic prowess. My mother had always driven us relentlessly to excel academically and to place greater value on amassing knowledge and information tempered by a healthy balance of faith more than obsessing on physical attributes we either possessed or lacked. My mother often said that any woman who used her brain to capacity was a beautiful woman, but not every beautiful woman turned out to be intelligent. Besides the Iron Lady herself, British Prime Minister Margret Thatcher had been known to have once remarked rather disdainfully that there was *'a nonsense about intelligent women not being beautiful.'* I had not known my sister Rose to have spent hours in front of the mirror preening herself more than she did in quiet, studious learning. Naturally when I was in high school my thirst for knowledge and my purposeful commitment to a life of faith led me in pursuit of academic success and a life of devoted prayer more than vain hours spent in search of external beauty and validation from my peers.

Every morning, for three years in high school I attended morning Mass at St. Paul's Seminary located next to the school. I had been quick to be friendly with the nuns running the convent and a young nun, Sister Grace had taken me under her wing. We would spend hours in discussion of life as a nun over lazy weekends and when she mentioned that she celebrated Mass daily I immediately expressed interest in joining her. And so it became my daily routine that every morning before lessons commenced for the day that we would take a short walk through a bushy woodland to the adjoining seminary for an hour of Mass celebration and prayer. I felt my desire to become a nun was a distinct calling. I had always known that I was a spiritual person-even more so now that I was deeply connected to sacramental worship rites of the Catholic religion and study of the Bible. I spent more time in prayer than I did worrying about how to make my friend Anthony, the good looking boy who lived two streets away from our home like me more than a friend. He was 17 years old with a dimple in his chin and every girl in my neighbourhood loved him and if he knew it he did not show it which only made him even more attractive. Modesty in a handsome young man who had the attentions of every pretty girl is a rare virtue.

The years flew by in a blur of study, prayer, Mass and more

studying. I managed to navigate the tumultuous years of adolescence without incident, successfully escaping the acne riddled drama of earnest renditions of young love so easily declared and just as quickly forgotten. I loved studying literature because I was genuinely intrigued by the human psyche and all the hidden layers beneath the seemingly banality of existence. Nuns could be University educated and Sister Monica was highly educated with training in education and child psychology. I wanted to be a highly educated nun too and my academic interest lay in social work. I wanted to help people; especially vulnerable individuals in families. As a qualified Social Worker I would be able to assist vulnerable children in high risk circumstances find safety and help them access all that was within their rights for their security and welfare. I had experienced first-hand the trauma of domestic violence, seen the damage it wreaked on us as we grew up in its terrifying shadow and I knew that I needed to play my part in order to end the cycle of cowardly silence by taking a stand for children living in violent homes. Perhaps the church would assign me to run an orphanage once I was qualified I mused. I loved the idea! I had a solid plan for my life and it would unfold perfectly. In 1993 my life took on a complete about turn. My father died on my 17th birthday.

Death is so final. Life slips into the darkness, never to be illuminated again. My father was gone. He was not simply gone because gone alluded to the possibility of returning. I would not hear his gravelly voice speaking, urging me to keep questioning life till I found the answers no matter how deeply shrouded they were in mystery. 'Don't be afraid to ask Shumi' he had said once in a rare moment of openness. 'Don't be afraid to change too' he had added as an afterthought. He failed to heed his own advice and adapt to a changing world and now he was dead. My father was dead as dead as any lifeless corpse would be. His breath stilled and his eyes dimmed forever. I would have to change too as I moved forward. If only I could move forward. I would have to learn to speak about what could have been without regret. Though he was alive in my mind, more alive than I had known him in the later years of his life, he was no longer going to be a part of my future. He had already missed out on so much of my life-the momentous meeting of the Pope, going off to high school and my decision to follow a calling of being a nun. There were so many memories he should have been a part of but those moments were lost forever.

'You are over bearing like your father.' they said when I would not change my mind. 'You ask too many questions; endless questions about anything and everything!' they snapped with irritation when I was curious. I had always been ashamed to carry traits and similarities to a man I had loved as my father as it wounded me deeply to know that I was truly my father's daughter. His memory while he lived was steeped in pain and regret and it hurt to be the one who mirrored him the most but now I found a small sense of comfort in knowing that I carried a part of who he was in me. I was the good part of him that used to live, the beautiful part that Mama fell in love with. I desperately wanted to remember him without resentment or rage but it was a struggle to forgive the man who had shattered our lives but now that he was gone I longed to hold on to memory of a father who loved me enough to see through my pain when he saw me stealing. Those were the memories that meant the world to me and the rest of the pain he had wrought in our lives I decided tearfully that I would seal the chronicles of his violence tightly shut that they could never be prised open again. If only life could be that simple.

I would not see his tall, strong frame filling a doorway as he returned from work. That is how I would remember him, how he had lived tall. He had lived tall in service to his countrymen, fighting for the freedom of a nation only to be locked up in a prison of self-inflicted isolation and shame when the world moved too fast for him to adapt to the change that was ultimately necessary for his survival. He had lived tall marrying the girl he loved and raising a family with her only to lose everything as happiness eluded him in a free but unfamiliar world. He had lived tall in pursuit of knowledge, teaching his children to seek knowledge without restraint but he did not live long enough to witness our success or celebrate our accomplishments. He was my father and yet he was also a stranger but a part of me yearned to remember him with honour. My father had lived tall and that is how I would immortalise him in my mind but a stranger had died instead, bowed and broken in his place.

A cold easterly wind blew across the desolate terrain as the coffin was slowly lowered into the ground. The cold seeped from the wet ground through my thin black pumps, numbing my toes. The chipped edges of the black stones adorning my shoes gleamed softly in the dim afternoon light. I stared at my shoes, counting the black stones. I fixed my eyes on the stones recounting them again, avoiding the descent of the coffin. I could not imagine that he was in that wooden box. It must be stifling to be in that box I thought as I stared at my shoes. It had rained incessantly since morning turning into a cold drizzle as the day wore on. The wind buffeted the thin coat I wore. I dug my hands deeper into the nylon lined pockets struggling to keep warm. The funeral service had been short. The eulogies were short and impersonal. It was a sad end for a man whose life could have been filled with more. A tear trickled down my cheek as it hit me again that my father was dead. When would I stop mourning I shuddered as we walked away from the pile of sand that marked his grave.

Maybe it was the fallibility of life that turned my heart. Or maybe it was the loss of my father whose life had not been lived to the very fullest of all he could ever have been. I began to question the meaning of the choices and decisions I had made for my own life. Choices that had seemed certain and morally sound right up until the news of his death. I had always known for a long time that I was destined to do something with my life that that would lead me to serve and love people and what better way to do that than selflessly giving up all material gain and pledging a lifelong commitment to ministry in service. I had committed to becoming a Social worker nun but now I yearned for more fulfilment in my chosen path. I knew I could no longer become a nun although I still desired to be a Social Worker. Something in me had changed, a restlessness that made me long for something different in my life. It was not dissatisfaction with my current life or even discontent. It was simply a yearning for more. I still prayed, I still spent time in meditative study of the Bible daily but the restlessness would not let me go. Some part of me felt incomplete and as I searched for fulfilment in more prayer and more study, the yearning did not dissipate. Three months after my father's death I stumbled on what I had been searching for.

Sometimes you know someone for what seems like a lifetime and yet you do not realise their significance in your life until one day when your heart misses a beat from just one look; a look that says everything and a look that means everything. The knowledge that I was in love came upon me suddenly during the first week of the winter holiday. I was sitting outside trying to catch the waning rays of the morning sun. Winters in the Midlands were brutal and the bleak glow of the sun through my bedroom window had lured me out onto the veranda with promises of warmth which were fading fast as I stood outside. It was not as warm as I had envisaged. The veranda was cold and draughty freezing my cheeks as I expelled the cold air from my lungs. Contemplating retreating into the house to my warm bed I saw him approach and he spotted me standing on the veranda and stopped.

'Hello Shumi! Long time.' Anthony called out.

'Hello stranger.' I waved back.

He opened the gate, walking towards me with a sombre expression I had not noticed until he was standing in front of me.

'I'm sorry about your dad Shumi. I heard the news of his passing from my mom when I got back from college.'

He squeezed my hand. My stomach lurched as suppressed pain rushed in waves and suddenly tears filled my eyes, spilling quietly down my face. Horrified I realised I was crying and angrily I brushed the tears away. He stepped towards me and quietly pulled me into his arms. It was an innocent gesture of comfort and yet I felt the tensile strength of his lean arms as he embraced me and my arms went around his broad back instinctively. His body felt warm and strong under my touch and I could smell the woody cologne off the jacket he wore. Suddenly I became acutely aware of his warm breath on my forehead. Startled I pulled away. His hands fell away from my shoulders and he awkwardly slipped them into the front pockets of his blue jeans, an imperceptible look on his angular boyish face.

Embarrassed I looked away as an interminable silence ensued between us. Why did I feel so strange I wondered? My body quivered slightly but it was not the cold. Raging and conflicting emotions coursed through my mind. I was both delirious and confused. I had felt an unfamiliar stirring in the moment my head had leaned on his chest and I heard the soft thud of his heart beneath his striped blue shirt and yet somehow it felt so right. But how could standing in the arms of a boy feel right? My mother had warned me about boys and I had never wanted to be with a boy until this very moment. Or had I suppressed my emotions, too afraid to fall in love with a boy who may one day hurt me? As I stood on the cold veranda outside the house my heart fluttered at the realisation that perhaps or maybe I was possibly in love with a boy who was none other than Anthony, the local heart-throb! A University student now, he was desired by most girls who lived in the neighbourhood. I knew I stood no chance against the hordes of beautiful girls throwing themselves at his feet. Besides I had known him for years now. He had not shown anything beyond friendly interest in me and our interactions had never evolved beyond casual if lengthy conversations about music. We were both huge fans of the soul musician Michael Bolton. We had exchanged music cassettes and other fan memorabilia in the past few years. I was a bona fide Bolton fan who wrote regularly to my music idol.

'How...How is College?' I stammered. He was a freshman at the University in the City, studying to be an accountant. He was well known and admired by many, the pride of our community.

'It's fine I guess.' he shrugged. 'I miss home though. Especially the people.' he said pointedly, his eyes keenly searching mine. Embarrassed again I looked away. What on earth did he mean by that? Was he suggesting he missed me? Why would he miss me? He probably meant his family I reasoned. Don't be a fool Shumi, I admonished myself harshly as the thoughts rushed through my mind. He is just your friend, do not get any ideas I warned myself sternly.

'You didn't miss me?' he probed, a smile dancing on his lips at my obvious bewilderment.

'No?! Nothing?! No sentimentality for me? Ouch Shumi!' he laughed as I shook my head.

'But I missed *you*. A great deal.' He said, suddenly serious again. Our eyes locked in a passing moment of an unspoken exchange. My heart yearned to decipher the look in his eyes as unspoken longing but Anthony would never want me I dismissed the thought as I looked away. More silence stretched out between us as the unspoken words hung in the air.

'You are really pretty Shumi,' his voice barely more than a low whisper as he moved closer. Unsure of what to do I looked at my feet. I was rooted to the ground, in my mother's yard where I had stood countless times with Anthony before with much to say, now dumb-struck, my mind a whirl of thoughts as I raked my mind for an apt reply that would not make me sound foolish or socially inept. Gently, he framed my face with his hands as he pulled me to face him. His fingers were cold against my skin but they felt like fire on my skin. The fire was spreading but I could not pull away, irresistibly drawn to him, compelled to yield to the spell he had cast over me. I did not want to pull away from what felt like home, here under his caressing gaze submerged in the deep pools of his brown eyes.

'Can I see you later Shumi?'

I nodded. He smiled and I noticed for the first time how his eyes danced when he spoke.

I saw him later that afternoon. We met at the corner park two streets away from home. We sat on a rocky ledge on the perimeter of the park opposite an imposing mast light that towered in the middle of the grassy patch. It was too early in the day for the lights to be on, even though it was an overcast day with dark clouds, but it was too cold for the children to be out at play so the park was deserted. The corner parks were municipal council designated green areas dotted throughout the densely populated suburb. In daylight young children swarmed the park for hours of play, safe from the busy streets with endless traffic streaming in and out of the suburb. As evening fell the lights turned night into day and the young teenagers would flock out to end the day chatting and laughing with friends or those they regarded to be more than just friends. Now I was sitting here with Anthony, a friend who had become so much more than just a friend in what seemed like a fleeting moment and yet a little less than eternity.

We sat in the park for three hours, deeply immersed in animated conversation. This time we spoke about more than our mutual love for soulful music. He told me about his new life in the City of Harare; about captivating lectures, long library hours and insurmountable deadlines for assignments that kept piling high. It was a heady world full of overscheduled daylight hours, sleep deprived nights and endless tutorials fuelled by caffeine and over the counter vitamins to stay afloat in a fast paced academic world. There was time for exploring and fun times too. Picnics, festivals and blaring music from portable stereos that filled many lazy weekends. I wanted to be part of this world too. Soon, I thought. I would be able to attend college and I too would be a part of the fun filled frenzy of attaining a higher education. There must be girls in this world too, I wondered, curiously unsure whether to ask him. It seemed so petty and childish to do that and as if he read my mind he glanced at me and smiled.

'Shumi, only you make me feel like I'm alive. And that I'm winning no matter how far I am from my goal. You push me to keep chasing goals and when I do something worth celebrating you admire me without the pressure of hero status. And I admire you too. I admire your courage and your grace. I love how you cling to kindness in a world that has stopped caring.' He paused to look at me with a renewed intensity. 'Other girls don't come close.' His voice trailed off. I had never been in love before but I knew without a doubt that this was near perfect. I was in love, a tender and young love, but love nevertheless. The kind of love that filled my head with day dreams of interlocked hands and stolen kisses. It made my head spin and my palms clammy in anticipation.

I met him many afternoons after that. And I listened as he spoke. I listened to his warm whispers and his deep throated laughter. I listened to his dancing eyes and smiling lips. I listened to his warm embraces and gentle touch. I listened to his soft kisses on my cheek and his shallow breathing as he held me close. I listened and I believed him. I believed him when his hand held mine and told me I was safe. I believed him when his gaze caught mine and his lips widened in a smile. I believed him when he leaned in and brushed his lips against my ear, whispering I love you Shumi. He was strong, intelligent and beautiful and he was mine. For four weeks of that winter holiday I was enamoured with the love I found in him and the love that burned brighter in me with each passing day. We took long walks in a familiar neighbourhood that seemed completely new, lost in our young love, our hearts ignited and aflame.

# CHAPTER 10

In literature class I had read a poem that spoke of finding contentment in life's blessings, often over-looked in our busy lives. It spoke of making room for the blessing of love. Not one to do anything in half measures I gave love a prominent seat in my life in the form of my beautiful Anthony. He was not only my friend, he was also my very heartbeat. The memories of all the pain I had been through as a child did not hurt as much anymore when I reflected on it because his presence in my life filled my heart with hope for love and beauty to overcome my broken past. He listened and he smiled. He did not grow tired of my endless chatter about life, plans and our future together. And he never stopped smiling when he would look at me. I smiled too, more than I had done in many years. My mother noticed the smile. She must have grown suspicious of my afternoon excursions with Anthony but I simply told her that he was helping me with academic plans for my future. What I did not tell her however was how he was an integral part of that future.

It was not entirely untrue that Anthony was assisting me to develop and attain academic goals. During the course of the year he helped me study whenever he was home; during mid-semester breaks or when the university was closed over the holidays. I had told him of my intentions of becoming a Social Worker because I wanted to help people. I wanted to offer hope and faith to wounded people drowning in desperate situations But l also wanted to do other things like most young people want to do, like travel—to distant worlds where I would discover new cultures and possibly find answers to the many questions I had pondered for years. I wanted to know the tide coming in to shore looked like. I wanted to hear the sounds of the ocean and to feel the sand running through my toes. I also wanted to feel snow on my skin. The answers I sought lay outside the borders of my homeland in worlds I had only read about. I yearned to experience the wonder of it all before I was married and had responsibilities.

During one of our many discussions Anthony had remarked that he knew of a way I could advance academically and at the same time satiate my wanderlust. He suggested that I join a youth corps for a few months before enrolling in a tertiary college to study for a degree in Social Work. He spoke of a global youth corps that helped marginalised communities through different activities. Largely dependent on volunteers, the major thrust of activities centred on building infrastructure to ensure hygiene, sanitation and food security. Young people were vital to delivering these goals. Anthony urged me to make an application to one well known youth corps organisation that operated internationally. The prospect of spending several months in a foreign land digging wells, building dam walls with other young people while training communities on sustainable food production, water conservation and environmentally friendly waste management practices was hugely appealing. I would finally be able to contribute meaningfully towards global issues and demonstrate true leadership through service as I had always desired growing up and I would do it all in a foreign land! I was excited!

A year after that magical winter holiday when our love story was birthed, I sat for my Ordinary Level examinations, which were the final secondary examinations in high school. I also made an application to participate in the youth corps' next expedition. The expedition was to be held in Cyprus, an island country in the Mediterranean in the following year. The full itinerary of the programme included ocean clean-up activities as well as training programmes on water pollution, prevention and conservation strategies. This would mean extensive travel along the coastline raising public awareness of water pollution, which if not brought in check, would adversely affect fishery production and tourism. The economy of the island country relied heavily on tourism, annually drawing in large crowds to its highly acclaimed coastal resorts and prominent historical archaeological sites. I envisioned balmy evenings watching the sun set on the Mediterranean listening to the crash of the waves as the tide pulled in. I imagined the feel of the sandy beach under my feet and the taste of salt in the air.

The idea of travel and service appealed to me but I knew that before setting sail on this journey to a sun drenched destination, with a noble mission to serve as well as sightsee, that I needed Mama's approval. No-one in our family had left Zimbabwe for foreign lands in pursuit of higher education or in missionary work before. My sister Rose, a qualified teacher, was resident in the country and so were all the cousins who had lived with us over the years. Although Aunt Jo regularly visited South Africa on frequent shopping trips, she had built her home here in her home country. She always confessed to Mama upon her return from her trips how she found it comforting to be back in her home, in her country of birth. Home is best she used to say as Mama nodded knowingly, in agreement. Would Mama ever accept my dream of travelling to a foreign land all the way across the continent to another continent, too far for her to visit me as she had done for so many years when I had been in boarding school? Mama would never let me go but I could not give up without trying. I had to try.

I found an unlikely advocate to plead my case before Mama from a least expected quarter, my sister Rose. It was late November and she had come to Gweru to attend a short training course at the local Polytechnic College in town for a few days. She had come alone, leaving her two daughters with her husband in Mazowe. One evening as we set about preparing for supper she asked me if I had any plans for my future now that my school examination results were to be released before next February. I wavered, uncertain if I should share my dream with her. Our relationship had always been precarious and the distance had not brought us any closer. I knew that some part of me loved her, she was my sister after all, but we were too different. How could I expect her to understand my desire to travel when she obviously preferred to live close to what was familiar? I had recently been informed that my application to be part of the Cyprus expedition had successfully passed the first round of screening. Out of thousands of applications I was overjoyed to receive news that I was proceeding to the next round of selection. This round included an interview in Harare with a panel of country representatives of the youth corps organisation.

Taking a risk, I decided to share my news with Rose. I needed to broach the subject anyway, because sooner or later the truth would have to be out.

'So you need to travel to Harare for the interview stage?' she asked when I finished. I nodded, my heart heavy. My secret dream was out. Would it be crushed? There was a momentary silence before she turned to me with a huge grin plastered on her face.

'Well done Shumi! I'm proud of you!' she exclaimed. 'You've done so much already all on your own!' She came to where I stood and hugged me tightly.

'I know it hasn't been easy for you Shumi. You're the one who had to take on the role of being Mama's helper and protector all these years and for you to decide to do this now is just a big decision. I'm here to support you. What do you need?'

I could hardly believe my ears. Was Rose saying she was supporting me? I had expected her to call it a hare brained idea and dissuade me with deriding remarks for being selfish. She did not say that. In fact, she thought it was a wonderful plan to travel the world before settling to study. I had not established where I was going to enrol for the social work studies because I rationalised that I needed to have fluid plans to allow for serendipitous events like a financial windfall in the form of a bursary or scholarship award to study in a foreign country after my expedition. I knew that a stint in a global youth corps would serve to greatly enhance my application to any university in the world, local or international.

Rose remarked the same. 'Shumi this opportunity will open up the world for you. The exposure, the experience and the global networks you'll develop as a result will be invaluable. She clapped her hands in delight as she stepped back and smiled at me.

'Have you told Mama about this?' she asked.

I shook my head. 'No I haven't told her yet. I don't know how to tell her' my voice trailed off.

'Don't worry Shumi, leave it to me.' she promised. 'Just give me all the correspondence you've received. I'll take care of this.'

She told Mama later that evening after supper. I was in the kitchen washing the supper dishes with Tinashe when Rose broke the news to Mama. I heard the resistance in Mama's voice as she questioned Rose but Rose held her ground and remained firm in her responses. Long after I had retired to bed with Tinashe I heard Rose slip into our dimly lit bedroom which we shared when she came to visit. Noiselessly she pulled on her bed clothes and slid into the empty bed next to mine.

'What did Mama say sis Rose?' I quizzed as I sat up in bed. Tinashe stirred next to me, breathing softly, sound asleep.

'You're still awake?' Rose whispered, surprised.

'I can't sleep. What did Mama say?' I pressed. 'She said no didn't she?'

Rose padded softly across the small room to my bedside and knelt in front of me. My heart sank. She was preparing me for bad news. Cyprus was not going to be a reality. It would stay a dream. I felt my heart thud in pain.

'No silly! Mama said yes!' Unexpectedly Rose was pulling me off the bed laughing as she twirled in the middle of our darkened bedroom. Breathlessly she proceeded to tell me about how Mama had finally capitulated.

'Mama was just scared that you'd be too far from home if anything should happen to you but after I told her that you'd have adult supervision she was willing to hear more about it.' She paused, lost in thought.

'Mama is in fact very proud of you Shumi and so am I.' she said with emotion in her voice.

Tears filled my eyes. This was more than I had ever dared to ask God for! Both Mama and Rose were proud of me and fully supported me!

'So I can go to Harare next month for the interview? I whispered, incredulous at the miracle taking place in my bedroom.

'Yes Shumi, next month you're going for the interview. It's really happening!'

I hugged her tightly as the tears streamed down my face in the dark.

# CHAPTER 11

**M**ama! Mama! The letter is here! It's here!' I screamed excitedly as I raced into the house, colliding with her in the open doorway. I had been watching the post over the past few weeks. I was expecting the interview results to come in by post. The interview had proceeded without incident. Four panellists seated across a wide pine table had asked various questions about who my role models were, what I considered to be memorable life defining moments and my views on faith and religion. I shared my passion for social justice and how I longed to pursue a degree in Social Work. I spoke about my moment in history welcoming the Pope while the world watched and how that historic moment had ignited a dream to reach the world through a life of service. I also spoke about my father and his lost dreams and how that had been the fuel that inspired me to chase my own dreams. They had nodded as I spoke, their expressions impassive as they probed deeper. After the interview they shook my hand and told me they would send their final decision in the post in the coming weeks. The letter was here at last.

'Open it Shumi!' Mama urged. Trembling I ripped the envelope open and pulled out a folded sheet of type written paper. With a silent prayer I turned it over, barely able to conceal the tumult of emotions surging through my mind as I rapidly scanned the letter.

'I made it Mama! I'm in! I'm going to Cyprus!' I shrieked as I threw the letter in the air.

A huge smile lit up her face as the reality of my words sank in.

'*Mwari vakanaka Shumi!*' (God is good Shumi!) She held my hands in hers and looked at me with a look of such love and pride in her tear-filled eyes. It was no longer a dream. It was no longer something I would only hope for. Fulfilment was at hand! Tears streamed down my face. She pulled me into her arms and we stood in the living room, sobbing till we were spent.

Anthony was overjoyed when he heard the news of my successful application. He had returned earlier that afternoon from University for a weekend visit. His visits were becoming a frequent occurrence lately, and he would justify his visits by admitting that he could not stay away from me. Visibly elated at the news he swept me up in his arms right there in the street outside my mother's house. Squealing with laughter I admonished him, pretending to be horrified at his display of affection in public. What would Mama say if she saw us I giggled, pulling away. After hugging me repeatedly and fist pumping the air several times he finally settled down to a quiet conversation. Consternation creased his features as it dawned on him that my good news meant separation for us, at least for several months.

'I'll miss you Shumi.' he said quietly. 'Don't get me wrong. I'm happy for you. It just breaks my heart that you will be gone for so many months.' He clasped my hands in his and looked searchingly in my eyes. I did not want to be sad now. I wanted to feel good because I was happy. There would be many occasions to be sad once we were apart. In this moment selfishly, I wanted to be happy, for me.

'I love you Anthony. Nothing could ever change that. We'll be ok if we trust that we will get through this.'

Going to Cyprus meant putting distance between us, distance that would separate us physically. The physical separation presented an opportunity for our relationship to be tested. Perhaps with the testing we would also grow. We had to deal with the unfamiliar and face the unknown with courage and faith if we wanted to grow. We would have to navigate the unknown terrain of a long distance relationship across two continents. I was ready to face the challenge of being apart from him if he was willing to hold on to our love through the difficult months ahead. The alternative of staying and not chasing my dream in a foreign land was too awful to comprehend. Our fingers intertwined we walked

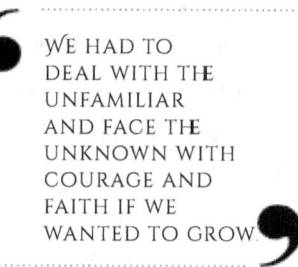

WE HAD TO DEAL WITH THE UNFAMILIAR AND FACE THE UNKNOWN WITH COURAGE AND FAITH IF WE WANTED TO GROW.

back home in silence, lost in thought as we held onto every minute we had left before we had to say goodbye.

The ensuing months were a whirlwind of activity of finalising all arrangements for the impending expedition to Cyprus. I was pleasantly surprised to discover that out of forty successful candidates, I was the only black African female applicant of four female applicants who made it to the final round. I met the other three girls at a meet and greet event in Harare organised by the expedition administrators. The event was meant to facilitate familiarisation of expedition rules and requirements as well as provide an opportunity to connect with other expedition volunteers. Aunt Jo accompanied me to the meet and greet and the following day she took me to the embassy to fill out my visa application. The flurry of packing for the trip began in earnest soon afterwards.

Three days before my flight was due to take off on the biggest adventure of my life my whole world collapsed around me. I had prayed fervently for this dream and my bags were packed, stacked in a neat pile in my bedroom against the wall, next to my bed. My passport with the newly issued visa was locked away in my mother's bedroom for safekeeping. I had told Tinashe about the expedition and though the news of my impending departure saddened her she looked forward to the gifts I would bring back for her from the trip. My mother had left for work earlier that day to fill in an application for two days leave from work so that she could accompany me to Harare to see me off at the airport. Aunt Jo was the one who would drive Tinashe, Mama and me to Harare and drive them back home afterwards. Rose was going to meet us in Harare on the day of my departure. I had spent the afternoon at home with Tinashe, cooking and cleaning, paying greater attention to my efforts in a bid to leave our home as clean as possible because I knew Mama and Tinashe would not have help taking care of all the domestic chores while I was gone. My mother walked in just before sundown, withdrawn and distant, with a worried expression on her face. Immediately I knew something was wrong.

As I cleared the supper dishes from the living room table later that evening she dropped the bombshell.

'Shumi I don't think it's a good idea for you to go to Cyprus.'

Stunned I dropped a plate I was holding onto the table with a loud clatter.

'Why? Why Mama?' I stammered, confused.

'I don't think it's safe for you to travel all the way to Europe with people I don't know.' She interjected. 'What if you don't come back.'

'But Mama...'I began to protest.

'But nothing Shumi!' She cut me off. 'I only have names and telephone numbers. I don't know these people! What if they are fake names and the numbers don't work after you've left for Cyprus? How will I find you?'

'They have offices in Harare Mama. You met the country representatives at the interview!' I wailed, barely able to conceal the anguish in my voice. 'There are students who have gone before and they came back. I met them. Aunt Jo also met them at the meet and greet session in Harare. You can ask her Mama.'

'I am your mother and Aunt Jo is not! I know best and I feel this is right for you. I am doing this to protect you Shumi! We will not discuss this anymore. My decision is final.' She stood up and left the room as I sobbed loudly.

All my carefully laid plans were shattered. Devastated I wondered what had made her change her already made up mind. Mama's final words hit hard. *My decision is final.* What did she mean that *her decision was final*? This was not about her life. It was about *my* life! I was going to be eighteen in a few months. I was practically an adult! How could she deny me a voice in deciding my own future? Did I not have a say in matters that affected my life? My future was wrapped up in the expedition that was now not meant to be according to Mama's proclamation! Distraught I rolled onto the floor as I my body shuddered in convulsive sobs. Why would she ruin my life by throwing away my dreams based on her irrational fears? Why was she taking this opportunity away from me? Why was she breaking my heart? Why did she hate me?! My mind unravelled in complete despair as I wailed on the living room floor.

When I had started out on this journey to fulfilling my dream I had known that the greatest obstacle would be my mother, but astonishingly, she had been supportive about my plans for months. Our broken relationship had been restored by her renewed faith in me in recent months. The pain of the wounds that existed between us still rankled beneath the surface but we were finally reaching across the distance in a gesture of acceptance and forgiveness. Tentatively I had begun to take steps on the broken path which connected us. I had noticed her eyes when she looked at me, as if she was seeing me for the first time and they were filled with pride. I felt accepted and I was whole again. She had even started praying about the trip, every evening at family prayer times, asking for God's protection to cover my life. Why would she be so cruel as to fan the embers of my dream every day for months on end only to dash my hopes so close to the day of fulfilment? Alone I lay on the living room floor and wept in the night.

# CHAPTER 12

If I secretly harboured any hope that somehow Mama would change her mind. I did not express it when Rose called the following morning to find out when we would be in Harare for my send-off. I numbly told her the trip was an unlikely possibility. Rose was adamant it was a temporary case of cold feet and that Mama was finding it hard to let me travel to a foreign land. She said she would speak to Mama and she told me not to worry. It was all going to be alright she promised. I did not believe her. I knew Mama only too well. She was stubborn and defiant. She had taken herself through high school when deeply rooted tradition had opposed her and stood in her way. Mama was a formidable force, an uncompromising adversary. My mother would get her way even when it seemed next to impossible. Besides I was also my mother's daughter. I understood that obstinacy only too well. Mama would prevail but what of the cost. I would soon find out.

Rose did speak to her and so did Aunt Jo but it was no use. Mama prevailed as I knew she would. I heard one end of their conversation when they called-which was mostly Mama asserting that she would not stand by and let me become a prostitute in the name of attaining an education. *Prostitute!* I was stunned! I later discovered that Mama's sudden about turn was a result of an inopportune conversation she had earlier with a colleague at work who had filled her mind with harrowing accounts of young girls used as sex slaves and drug mules overseas. In a desperate bid to prevent the same fate befalling her daughter Mama had shut the door on my dreams without another thought. She would not listen to my frenzied pleas or acknowledge my anguished tears, rationalising that I would see the wisdom of her decision in the future when I was older and perhaps even thank her. She would not consider that the organisation organising the expedition was a reputable Christian based agency which had many years of experience. Everything I had done in the past year had been building up to the expedition to Cyprus, not only because it was a trip to a foreign destination but also because I saw this as a necessary step towards liberty from a limiting past. I would finally be breaking free from the wounds of my past and building towards my future. Mama would no longer hear of it, her decision was final.

At first I was devastated and then my pain gave way to a seething anger. My rage festered, fuelled by the unfairness and injustice of the decision Mama had made without a second thought to the impact it would have on me. I had trusted her and she had betrayed that trust. I had trusted my father too and he had had ripped our lives apart with his murderous rage. Trusting the people I loved dearly only gave them room to hurt me deeply. Mama had also ripped out my heart when she denied me the right to dream for myself. She was bound in her own prison of fear, wrought by her loss of faith in the basic decency of humanity, and she was holding me hostage to her fear. I wanted to live with purpose, to leap out in uninhibited expectation and curious anticipation of life's opportunities and to live without regret but that required faith which she had lost many years ago shattered on the living room floor in a home she had lived with a man locked in his own prison of fear and rage.

I understood her concerns for my safety but her irrational fear was stifling *my* dreams and *my* future. I was angry and my anger led me into a dark world of hopelessness and silence. I did not know how to stem the tide of rage that was smouldering inside me and to keep my feelings at bay I grew silent. I hardly spoke to Mama except to acknowledge her in the mornings when we met in the kitchen or to respond to a question she had asked. I avoided her and when carrying out my chores I would wait for her to leave the room first. My prayers also grew silent and I stopped praying, my words cut short by a pain I could not express coherently. I had no words left to say to Mama and I did not understand why God had permitted the crushing disappointment and despair of my broken heart. So I kept silent and isolated in my pain the rift in our relationship deepened. She tried to span the distance with quiet conversations about making other plans for my future but the distance between us was too wide and besides it was too soon. I was too angry to forgive her.

The anger seeped into my relationship with Anthony, crushing the promising bloom of our young love beneath its pervasive weight. He wanted me to begin making plans for an alternative future but I could not easily get over my stolen dreams. To consider anything else felt like a betrayal of all that I had hoped for. I was not ready to make walk away from my dreams. We struggled to talk and soon we began to fight about everything. The darkness of my anger put more distance between us than could be bridged. The final death knell came four months after my bitter disappointment.

He was home for two months on the long semester break before classes for the next academic year resumed at the University. Tentative plans for our afternoon walk had been made the day before but I had been non-committal. We had not taken our usual afternoon walk for several weeks. When he came home after midday to fetch me, he found me distant and indifferent to his efforts to persuade me to join him in taking a short walk to the park at the end of the street. I did not feel like taking a walk. I was uncompromising and his pleas fell on deaf ears. Feeling sorry for myself I returned to my bed where I had become accustomed to spending many solitary afternoons.

After fitfully sleeping all afternoon I woke up to my room awash with light from the golden rays of a late afternoon sun streaming through my open window on its western descent. Perhaps it was the promise of a glorious sunset or perhaps my heart had softened after the long afternoon nap, I reflected on how caring and compassionate Anthony had been throughout my ordeal but how I had repaid his kindness with selfishness and more thoughtlessness. After splashing water on my sleep lined face I made my way to Anthony's house, two streets away from home. If I hurried I would be able to see him for a few minutes and apologise for my sour disposition, getting back home before the darkening streets were illuminated in the electric glow of the massive tower mast light at the end of the street. Nearing the end of the street my heart fluttered as I thought of his lean arms holding me and how he made me feel safe. How could I have been so cold to him I wondered to myself shaking my head. I did not deserve him, I thought as I turned the corner.

I froze in my tracks, less than five yards from me Anthony was walking with a beautiful fair skinned girl I knew as Bridget. Her face upturned to his, she was laughing at something he had said and losing her footing she stumbled. Reaching out to steady her, she held onto his outstretched arms and I noticed the way his arms held her lithe body in his and how she leaned in closer, willing him to hold on to her. The way I felt when he held me too. My heart constricted as I stood there rooted to the ground. As if sensing my watchful eyes on them, Anthony looked up and on seeing me in the street, he stepped back quickly letting Bridget go in the same quick movement. He smiled awkwardly as he walked towards me.

'Shumi, I did not see you' he stammered. 'What are you doing here?' embarrassment registered in his voice.

'Obviously the surprise is on me' I responded acidly.

Bridget smiled, a flash of perfect white teeth. She was strikingly beautiful with big, doe-eyed brown eyes set in a near perfect face. She had delicately boned features with luminous skin that glowed as though made of liquid gold. I knew she was a freshman at the Polytechnic college in town. I had always known that Anthony was desired by many beautiful girls. His boyish good looks and charm were a lethal combination that made him irresistibly appealing but I had always trusted him to fend off unwanted female attentions. Though confident in my own skin, my version of beautiful paled in comparison to Bridget.

'See you tomorrow Tony.' Bridget called out, an unmistakable and bold hint in that promise. She turned away and gracefully sauntered into the lengthening shadows.

'Shumi it's not what you think.' Anthony began.

'It's never what I think' I broke in. 'You're standing here with Bridget looking like two starry eyed lovers and it's not what I think. It's not what I think when my own mother destroys my dream because she does not want me to travel and see the world. It's not what I think when my whole world falls apart around me and I'm so angry and I don't know how to move from here. I'm stuck and I'm scared about where my life is going but here you are with another girl and you're telling me it's not what I think!! You're obviously moving on!'

'I haven't moved on Shumi!' he retorted. 'But I agree with you on one thing. You're angry and you're stuck. Just today you didn't want to come out for a walk with me and you have refused to do anything for weeks now. Nothing I do seems to help or change how you feel about things.'

'I'm here now aren't I?! I'm trying! I changed my mind and I'm here now but you're chasing other girls already!' I sobbed.

He reached out to take my hand but I pushed him away.

'If you wanted to help Anthony then you shouldn't have tried to make me feel guilty for the way I feel. These are my feelings and I have every right to feel every emotion until I'm ready to move forward. What I am going through is not pity party. I am hurting and I can't pick myself up when it suits you and carry on like my heart was never broken.'

'Your heart is so broken that you don't have room to choose anything or anybody else Shumi.'

Profoundly shaken I was momentarily silent. It was true I thought, my heart was broken, maybe too broken to continue on a charade of what my sister Rose called puppy love. This was real life and I was facing the giants of disappointment and crushing hopelessness. I felt defeated because I was constantly losing. Even now I was losing Anthony. Our love could not withstand the storms of my brokenness. Like the opportunity to pursue my dreams in Cyprus that had slipped through my fingers at the very last moment, I felt a door was closing on my heart's love. I had been stuck for many weeks since Mama had stood in the way of the fulfilment of my dreams but I did not have to stay stuck anymore.

I was still breathing and with every breath I took I could choose something different, something better. Not all my choices were going to be of apocalyptic proportions, of my me versus the world. Some choices would be simple and yet others complex. I knew that I was going to be called upon to make decisions about the future I wanted and some of the choices I would make would look like I was trading my dreams for lesser options. Whether I was downsizing or upgrading my dreams I would always have to remember to choose what was truly important to me. Sometimes it takes losing something precious to discern that all is not completely lost. In some cases, what remains is something else of value, perhaps even greater value than what was lost, something valuable like my freedom. As I stood in the evening light I realised that in every loss there is something gained. I had lost Anthony but I remained and I was worthy. I would have to remind myself of this truth in later years.

'You're wrong Anthony' I replied 'I have a choice and I choose myself because I am worthy of more. You've made your choice and I wish you well. Good bye Anthony'

I had not imagined that my heart could be broken again when it was already shattered. I cried myself to sleep that night and several nights after that. I missed Anthony terribly and the memories of our love haunted me chasing sleep and rest. I cried into my pillow to muffle the sound of my weeping. My heart bled as the days stretched out into what seemed like an eternity. About a month later the tears stopped and I did not wince when I thought of him. That is when I knew I was becoming stronger. I had to keep busy and so I threw myself into a busy routine of cooking, cleaning and assisting Tinashe with her school homework. In perfect timing as though in answer to an unspoken prayer I was called for an interview at a teacher training college in Masvingo. Unbeknown to me Mama had applied for a place to study at the teacher's college on my behalf when she saw a posted advertisement in the press. When my application was selected for an interview she had to come clean, fervently hoping that I would be willing to attend the interview. To her complete surprise and amazement, I agreed to attend the interview. I needed a new outlook on life and moving away from home to a college in another city would provide me with the time and space to find healing in new beginnings.

# LOVE

"AND NOW ABIDE
FAITH, HOPE, LOVE,
THESE THREE, BUT
THE GREATEST OF
THESE IS LOVE."

(1 CORINTHIANS 13:13)

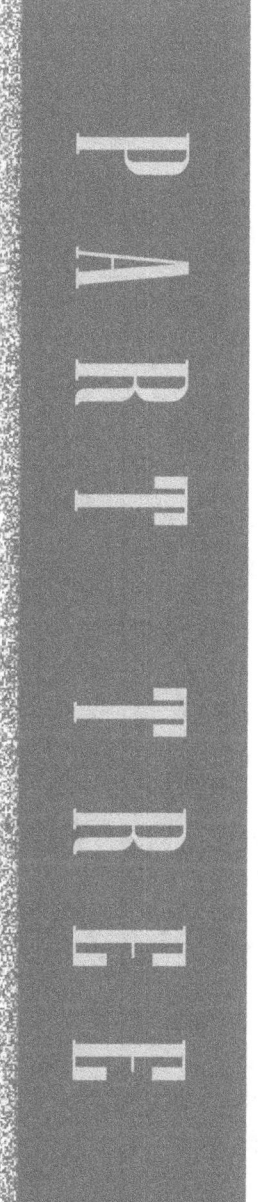

PART TREE

# CHAPTER 13

At 19 I was enrolled in college in Masvingo. College was a gratifying experience of self-discovery and independence. After receiving news of my successful application to study at the teacher training college I had begun the process of preparing for the next chapter of my life; life as a college student. My mother who was more acquiescent to my demands was very encouraging as I prepared for college life, taking on a new direction in my academic life. Although I still yearned to be a social worker I was willing to explore the long route to my purpose. I loved that I would still be working with children, in a different context but I could still reach those that needed comfort, protection or help while I was teaching. Divine Providence had made it possible once again for me to reach for my dreams. I was on the right path. I rationalised that after a few years spent in the teaching profession I could always go back to college to study for a qualification in Social work after the completion of my teacher training diploma. I was confident that combined with my teaching experience I would be an instrumental asset in any organisation providing Social work services.

Life on campus was busy and demanding as it was interesting. Classes started early in the morning on weekdays and continued till late in the afternoon. Alternate afternoons were set aside for sporting activities for all classes. Lectures were taxing and expectations of the academic staff were high. Soon life became a blur of classes, tutorials and group discussions. Evenings were taken up with endless assign-ments and more group discussions. The frenetic pace of life on campus only slowed down on Friday afternoons as the weekend drew near. Weekends were the only opportunity to pause and wind down in preparation for the coming week. My Friday afternoons were spent in my room catching up with much needed sleep. The days slipped into weeks.

Growing up I made friends easily and college was no surprise. My roommate Esther was my first friend but soon I had a clique of five girls who became my close friends. We spent much of our free time together chatting and laughing. However, as the weeks turned into months we began spending less time together as one by one, each girl found herself in a relationship, usually with an older boy. Esther's boyfriend, Gary, lived in Bulawayo and she spent many weekends in Bulawayo visiting her boyfriend. Left to my own devices I spent many weekends in bed reading paperback African love stories or sleeping. On occasion I would be downstairs on Saturday afternoons waiting for the public phone booth, for a call from either Mama or Rose. Those telephone calls were the mainstay of my connection with my family. They usually called on Saturday afternoons and sometimes when I was dozing off on my bed, taking an afternoon nap, I would hear fellow residents screaming in the corridors for me to hurry to the phone.

One Saturday morning just after breakfast I was called to the phone. Surprised that my mother had decided to call uncharacteris-tically early I rushed downstairs to the waiting phone. Maybe some-thing was wrong. I slipped into the phone booth, closing the door softly behind me. I picked up the phone. A male voice responded.

'Who is this?' I queried, surprised. Had someone mistakenly called me downstairs to receive a call that was not mine I wondered.

'You don't know me but I know you Shumirai.' His slightly accented voice was deep and smooth. 'My name is Vusi.' he continued. I listened as he told me how he had seen a photograph of me in the possession of his friend in Bulawayo and he knew instantly that he needed to speak to me. The photograph in question was one Esther had given to her boyfriend Gary, the afore-mentioned friend who lived in Bulawayo. It was a photograph of Esther and me, looking the picture of summer beauty in our floral dresses as we smiled in the sun lounging on the well-manicured lawn of campus grounds. Vusi was Gary's friend. Intrigued by his cultured and yet sultry voice I conversed with him for half an hour until we were interrupted by incessant knocks on the phone booth door. I was reminded then of the queue of girls waiting outside the phone booth waiting their turn to use the phone. Smilingly told him I needed to terminate our conversation.

When I told Esther about Vusi she squealed with delight. Elated that I was finally in the sights of someone of the opposite sex she celebrated my new 'relationship' by buying a candy bar for me from a nearby kiosk. She knew of my love for sweet treats. 'Sweet wishes to start of a sweet relationship' she had said with a wink. Laughingly I told her it was hardly a relationship, more than it was a simple conversation between two strangers. All I knew about him was that he lived in the resort town of Victoria Falls in the northwest region of the country. He was employed as an administrator in a touring company based there. Apart from his seductively riveting voice I had no way of knowing what he looked like I pointed out. She dismissed my sentiments as inconsequential and knowingly added 'You'll see Shumi.' Soon enough, next Saturday morning he called again and so began our phone booth conversations. We spoke at length about different things from our favourite traditional dishes to our shared disdain for politics, lists of must read books, our mutual desire to travel and our love for music. I began looking forward to Saturday mornings.

Four weeks after our phone booth conversations started I leapt at the invitation to visit Vusi in Victoria Falls when he suggested I travel the next weekend. He made arrangements to send money for my travel to Victoria Falls. The two leg journey to the resort town was long but I hardly noticed, too excited at the prospect of finally meeting Vusi. I weathered the noisy four-hour bus ride to Bulawayo in a state of anxiety and euphoria. After a brief stop in Bulawayo to board a connecting bus to Victoria Falls, I was soon on my way. Eight hours later I arrived in Victoria Falls as twilight heralded the descent of the sun.

Vusi was waiting at the bus station when the bus drove into the bus station. Head and shoulders above the teeming crowd of travellers he had smiled when he spotted me curiously scanning the crowd for a man I did not know by sight. He was powerfully built with strong, sculpted arms and broad shoulders. His gold flecked brown eyes were deep set in a face with high planed cheek bones, full lips and a broad sloping forehead. He was even more handsome than I had dared to imagine. Suddenly feeling inadequate as I thought of my own plain looks in comparison, I shied away when he tried to embrace me. Unperturbed he held my hand in his and smiled broadly as his eyes keenly swept over my face, oblivious to my growing discomfort.

'You're truly even more beautiful in real life my chocolate queen,' he murmured softly as I shyly averted my eyes from his penetrating gaze.

'Let's go home,' he said, deftly pulling the overnight bag I was carrying from my shoulder with his other hand. With my hand firmly grasped in his, he led me out of the crowded bus station.

Home was a sparsely furnished three roomed apartment in a complex of identical semi-detached buildings on the outskirts of the residential area in the resort town. It consisted of an open plan kitchen-cum-living room with two doors leading off into a clean if small bedroom and a tiny bathroom with sea green walls comprising a shower and a toilet seat. The living room furniture consisted of a set of hard backed wooden chairs and a small oval side table. A neatly made double bed prominently took up space in the bedroom. A dresser with a mirror was placed against the pastel painted wall next to a floral print curtained window in the small room.

That first evening he insisted that I rest and with a flourish he pulled up one of the living room chairs and playfully ordered me to take a seat until he was done preparing our supper. So I sat on a chair laughing at his quick wit as he regaled me with stories that kept me riveted on this charming handsome man who was adept in the kitchen. That he was also confident in his masculinity enough to display his culinary skills and his obviously high housekeeping standards only intrigued me. I had never heard of a man who would willingly cook for a woman! He prepared a spicy dish of pan fried fresh bream from the Zambezi River and piping hot *sadza*, a thickened corn meal mash served with steamed leafy greens. After supper he cleared the dishes and made two cups of hot black tea. We sat in the living room and spoke long into the night till the tea grew cold, untouched on the table.

'Vusi it's 3am!' I exclaimed in surprise glancing at my watch.

He laughed, a rich melodic timbre that filled the small room. 'It is indeed! You need to rest.'

With that he stood up and walked into the bedroom. My heart fluttered in fear. I had worried about this very moment. Would he suggest that I share his bed? And what would his reaction be if I declined his overtures to seduce me? I had travelled halfway across the country to meet with him but I had no intention of giving myself to a man, no matter how bewitching his charm, before marriage. For many years I had believed that I was going to be a nun, fully embracing the significance of the vows I would take, including the vow of chastity. My mother had instilled in me a deep sense of pride in upholding age old traditions of purity before marriage in an evolving world which had discarded those same values. My decision to stay chaste was my right and my choice, intertwined and inseparable with my identity and my self-will, a symbol of the power I had in my control in determining my choices and choosing my destiny. Not just over my body but also over every other aspect of my life. This liberty was enshrined in my freedom to choose what I perceived was befitting for my life. The reality though was a far cry from the truth. I knew I had a right to choose but I was also a woman. I understood all too well how easily that liberty could be taken away.

The vulnerability of women in our communities had been raised at a prominent international conference that had made waves globally the previous year in 1995. Women from Zimbabwe joined thousands of other women from all over the world  in China at the Beijing Declaration and Platform for Action of the Fourth World Conference on Women, adding their voices in a call to action to protect the rights of women and girls and to eliminate all forms

> THE WINDS OF CHANGE HAD BEGUN BLOWING BUT THE REFORMS WERE SLOW TO COME.

of abuses upheld by customary law or tradition. The winds of change had begun blowing but the reforms were slow to come. It saddened me to hear that barely five years after the Beijing Declaration, girls were still denied an education in many families with their brothers placed ahead of them in resource distribution. Reforms to inheritance laws for widows were not applied especially in rural Zimbabwe where change was unwelcome. The status of women in Zimbabwe and in the world for that matter still ranked marginally lower than their male counterparts. The threat of violence against women in both public and private was also an ever present reality. I knew too well the effects of that violence.

He walked out of the bedroom with a sleeping bag and a pillow slung over his shoulder.

'The bed is ready Shumi.' He announced. I'll sleep here in the living room.' Hiding my surprise at his chivalry I smiled my thanks as he tossed the sleeping bag and pillow on the floor. I moved towards the bedroom door brushing past him as he prepared his floor bed. He reached out pulling me close and tenderly his lips brushed mine.

'Goodnight Shumi,' he whispered as he turned away and slid into the sleeping bag. I walked into the bedroom and softly closed the door behind me.

# CHAPTER 14

The months sped by amidst the busy routine of lectures, assignments, presentations and weekly phone booth conversations with Vusi. Once every month I would travel to Victoria Falls to visit him. With each visit I became more certain of my deepening feelings for Vusi. I expectantly awaited each weekly phone call. He was opinionated and intelligent and we sparred at length in intellectual debates. But I especially looked forward to the monthly visits. He was generous, considerate, respectful and always mindful to make my comfort his priority. We spent many daylight hours sight-seeing in the resort town. I remembered the awe inspiring feeling that stirred in me the first time I had seen the magnificent thundering waterfalls. He had taken me back several times on subsequent visits. I never tired of hearing the roar of the Zambezi River rushing down the steep ravine and getting drenched from the fine spray. The evenings routinely ended with a goodnight kiss as we parted at the bedroom door.

Vusi knew that I was passionate about education and empowerment of women. That he did not feel threatened by my position on equality of women only served to endear him further. Most of the male students in my class would resort to calling me a feminist when I spoke about how women were notable contributors to economic productivity in the world. I argued that through provision of labour, imparting direction and wisdom in harnessing the family unit they had made considerable contributions to establishing structures from the Stone Age to modern economies in the 20th century. I did not make provision for a growing realisation, that strong-willed women were unpopular. The former female premier of the United Kingdom, Margaret Thatcher was a case in point. I was frustrated at the label of feminism. I was a human being just as much as I was a woman and I was here for the truest expression of self regardless of gender. How could I be unrestrained in pursuit of my dreams when I was shackled by archaic perceptions on what a good woman was? I had no patience for old oppressive ways that had no place in a new way of life. Even the Bible spoke of a God who did new and extraordinary feats. I was deeply pleased that Vusi agreed with me.

How deep my feelings were for Vusi was revealed during a visit to Victoria Falls, six months after our first meeting. As we prepared for bedtime in what I now called my second home, I stood in the bedroom doorway and kissed him goodnight as was customary each night. Only this time instead of turning away I stood in the open doorway. Unable to voice my decision, made hastily in the moment, I became a willing victim of my own passions. Looking up from where he had rolled out his sleeping on the floor he saw me framed in the dimly lit open doorway and he understood what was left unspoken. He strode to where I stood and silently led me into the bedroom.

Our union was both simple and beautiful. The novelty and intensity of our vulnerability in the moment overshadowed any lingering shame I felt. He held me in his arms and asked me at every turn if I was comfortable. I felt him stiffen once as he encountered momentary resistance and surprise flashed in his eyes as he looked into mine.

'You're a virgin,' he whispered tenderly. I nodded silently, too afraid to speak, too afraid to ruin the moment with my guilty thoughts. His arms tightened around me gently as though to protect me from my shame and any vestiges of doubt or regret vanished. Later with tears in his eyes he asked me to marry him. I laughed. We have time Vusi I said. But time was running out.

A week later I was back in Victoria Falls. Unable to withstand the time and distance that separated us, I had welcomed the idea of visiting him at the end of the week instead of waiting till the end of the month for our customary monthly visits. Our relationship, no longer platonic, had transcended the physical boundaries that had existed before. I had opened the door to a burning need that had become a sea of flames I could no longer suppress. I had no experience in this physical turn in our relationship. I was unprepared for the all-consuming effect. Sister Monica had spoken of the fires that burned for those who gave room to sin. She had not warned me of how willingly I would want to be cast in the furnace of desires I could no longer control. There was no hope for those who flagrantly danced with sin. I had started the dance, dangerous and unfamiliar, but I was not willing to stop. Immersed in the throes of my dance I turned away from the values I had held for all my life. The truth I had learned as a growing child wrestled with new yearnings I discovered as a young woman. Besides, the inspiration for my evolution was love. I loved Vusi deeply and truly, and if love was a requirement to justify the choices I had made then I was not too far from the truth.

I made the decision to visit Vusi a day earlier than we had planned. This meant that I would miss a full day of lectures on Thursday but the prospect of a longer weekend with him was a price I was willing to pay in lieu of missed classes. But I had to cover my absence because the college frowned upon cutting classes and some of the lecturers took attendance seriously; seriously enough to fail a student if one missed classes unnecessarily. Not willing to besmirch my good record I knew I had to feign sickness in order to avert suspicion on my absence in class. On Wednesday morning I attended class, withdrawn and somewhat subdued. Not known for my reticence during lectures, the tutors soon noticed and expressed concern at my ill looking state. My performance proved better than I had dared hope when one tutor suggested that I stay in bed the following day.

I was up much earlier than usual on Thursday morning preparing for my journey to Victoria Falls. I wore his favourite dress, a vibrant purple dress, the one I had worn in the photograph that Vusi had first seen me. To keep warm, I threw on my thick black jersey as I headed out. I decided to hitch hike to Bulawayo early in the morning instead of getting a bus, in order to get to Bulawayo sooner. That way I would be in Bulawayo in time for the midday bus to Victoria Falls. By 5am I was on the Masvingo highway, alongside other travellers, flagging down passing traffic. Within minutes a single cab truck heading to Bulawayo stopped. Hurriedly I jumped into the front seat, squeezing onto the narrow seat with another passenger while two other travellers jumped into the canvas covered back. The truck sped into the mist covered morning, making very good progress. I arrived in Bulawayo by 9am, just in time to board a newly introduced mini bus to Victoria Falls. 5 hours later I arrived in Victoria Falls.

Checking the time, I realised that I would find Vusi home if I walked briskly to the complex of apartments where he lived. I knew he was usually home for lunch and happily lost in thought I wondered what he had prepared for lunch. Vusi was an excellent cook and I always enjoyed his meals, especially his fish meals. Glancing at the cloudless blue sky as I walked up to the door, I was filled with excitement at the long weekend that stretched out invitingly before me. I tried the door. It was unlocked. Gently I pushed it open. The living room was empty. A pot simmered quietly on the stove in the kitchen. The aroma of garlic and rosemary filled the room. I smiled. He was home. The bedroom door was slightly ajar. Loud soulful music wafted from the bedroom into the living room. He had recently bought a blue and silver music player complete with 4 speakers, a sub-woofer, a six compact disc changer and two cassette player stereo. He was very proud of his newly acquired sound system. He was playing his favourite Lionel Richie album. Smiling I pushed the door open.

He was lying in bed, on his back while she lay next to him on her side listening intently to what he was saying. Loud music filled the room. My heart constricted painfully as the room darkened and swayed before me. My mind recoiled in horror at the memories of Vusi and I in this very room on that bed, only days before. Confused and blinded by pain I stood in the doorway, my smile frozen in a grotesque twisted crack. Sensing my presence in the room Vusi turned his eyes towards the door, inhaling sharply as he shot upright in bed. Following his gaze, she turned too and instinctively she reached for her clothes which lay in a heap on the floor. Her terror filled eyes darted towards Vusi. I ran out of the room sobbing, picking up my bag from the table in the living room where I had placed it. I needed to leave this scene of betrayal and hurt. I needed to get out! Vusi raced after me, catching me in the living room as I stumbled towards the door.

'Shumi I'm sorry! Please don't leave! Please!' he pleaded as he pulled me back. Hot angry tears streaming down my face, I pushed him away. His powerful arms drew me in. 'I'm sorry. I'm sorry Shumi' dazed, he kept repeating. Pulling me to a chair he knelt before me, wiping my tears as they fell. Shuddering he held me as he cried too. Please don't leave Shumi. I'll do whatever you want. Please don't leave,' he sobbed. Through tear filled eyes I saw the bedroom door swing open as she slipped out, passing us quietly in the living room she quickly walked to the door. I wept inconsolably as the door closed softly behind her. My heart was shattered and bleeding, ripped open by a man who had been the centre of my world. I ached at the lie I had lived all these months, believing that I was his treasure but in reality he had cared very little for me. I had given my all in exchange for heartbreak and devastating betrayal.

His lips moved. He was speaking but only a loud scream filled my ears. I could not hear what he was saying. I was drowning in a sea of pain, submerged under waves of bitter anger and desperate heartache. I closed my eyes. I would not look at his face, at those liquid brown eyes swimming in guilt. I would never let him lie to me again! The screaming in my ears grew louder and suddenly he was shaking me, fear and concern in his eyes. I opened my eyes and I stopped screaming. The room grew silent. Lyrics from the music playing in the bedroom drifted into the living room. Convulsive sobs wracked my body as a flood of raw emotion filled my wounded heart. Our love was crushed under the weight of a dark shadow that threatened to engulf my life. I spun in the darkness, desperately broken and hopeless. I had given too much, far too much; much more than I could hope to get back. Mama had always said that only within the confines of marriage could one expect and even demand fidelity. Only within marriage could one never give too much because on the marriage bed was true sacrifice, a total giving of oneself to the other. This is why virtue in a bride or groom before marriage was necessary she had said. To protect the union because outside these confines lay a minefield of immorality and debauchery that would destroy lives. I gasped for air as the tears fell. I had made an awful mistake.

The smell of burning filled my nostrils. The pot on the stove! Vusi rose to his feet, rushing to the kitchen. He grabbed the pot from the stove and threw it into the sink. An acrid smell filled the air as the pot spewed black smoke. Dazed he looked at the blackened pot as he glanced at his watch.

'You must be hungry Shumi.' His voice was hoarse and strained.

Without waiting for my response he walked back into the bedroom emerging seconds later with his wallet in hand.

'I'll be back in 20 minutes. I need to get some food for you to eat.'

Haltingly he moved towards the door turning to look back at me, a forlorn figure standing in the open doorway. He opened his mouth to say something then motioning helplessly he shut the door softly behind him. I sat in the empty house. The afternoon sun cast lengthening shadows into the room. The music had stopped playing and an eerie silence filled the emptiness in the room, echoing the aching emptiness I felt. I waited a few minutes and picking up my bag from the floor I walked out.

I spent the journey back to Bulawayo in complete silence. Avoiding the bus station where I knew Vusi would look for me, I had headed for the highway that led out of town. Shortly after arriving at the pedestrian stop where a few travellers gathered for the same purpose, a green mini-van had stopped in front of me. With a trio of other travellers, I slid into the backseat of the van. As soon as the vehicle had driven onto the road I settled into the bucket shaped seat and closed my eyes. To my companions in the in the van I appeared as though I was asleep but in reality behind my closed eyes my mind raced wildly. Fleeting images of Vusi with the unknown woman were seared in my memory. My eyes flew open. I had to be strong and to keep my emotions at bay somehow until I was alone. I quickly wiped the tears rolling silently down my face.

After promising to choose myself I had somehow managed, yet again, to be in this position of having my confidence and trust betrayed by someone I loved dearly. Vusi's infidelity struck me at the core in a way I had never felt before and yet this place was familiar. I had been in this place of crippling pain and broken hearted torment before. Was there something wrong with me? Was I unworthy of love? I thought of my mother and the ache I felt for the father who had never been present. The wounds of my broken childhood surfaced as I struggled to hold back the tears. Vusi's violation was like a knife plunged deep in my heart. His infraction had set me adrift and I felt utterly alone in the world. Something inside of me died as the car sped on its way, taking me further and further away from where my heart had bled. I slumped deeper into the seat. When would this cycle of rejection ever end?

We drove into Bulawayo just after dusk. I stood on the pavement, alongside the thoroughfare that was the highway to Masvingo. A few other travellers stood on the roadside, flagging down passing vehicles. Night was falling fast across the city. Anxiously I stepped onto the road and frantically waved as vehicles approached from the direction of the traffic lights that had just turned green. A white Toyota pulled up alongside the darkened curb. The driver was heading to Masvingo. I jumped into the vehicle along with four other travellers. It was just after 8pm when the car sped out of Bulawayo.

As the car wound its way on the moonlit highway I slipped into silence again. The travellers conversed quietly with the driver. Soft music played on the radio CD player. My body ached from the more than 12-hour journey I had endured since 5am that morning. I awoke to the car slowing down just outside a small mining town, Mashava, 50 km from Masvingo. The quartet of travellers disembarked. They had arrived at their destination and with loud profuse thanks they vanished into the darkness as the car pulled off into the night. I glanced at the time in the luminous dial reflecting on the dashboard. It was a quarter to midnight.

A quarter moon hung in the sky as a few clouds drifted slowly past. The Toyota swerved to the left, moving off the road and into the shoulder of the road on a patch of soft gravel and dry brush banked up on that side. The driver turned off the ignition. I sat upright peering into the night wondering why he had stopped. The door on my left opened and suddenly I was being dragged out violently.

'What are you doing,' I screamed hysterically.

I kicked desperately as he continued dragging me through patchy scrub brush and overgrown wild grass towards an enclave of trees just beyond the deserted road. Hidden from view behind the thick foliage he threw me down onto the hard unyielding earth. The moon cast its silvery glow on the tree tops and his eyes glinted in the moonlight. Suddenly his malicious intentions were clear. I fumbled in the dark feeling for something to use to fight back, despair rising as only loose soil filled my hands. I scrambled backwards as I tried to rise but he pinned me down with his powerful grip and his shadow slid down in the darkness. Moments later a searing wave of pain rippled through my body as the screams died in my throat. It was too late. I was too late. I was too late to see the danger. It was too late to escape. It was too late to undo the events of the past week. I was far too late! I shut my eyes as I lay limp on the gravel cutting into the small of my back. The moon hid behind a cloud and darkness settled over the tree tops. The scent of eucalyptus hung in the still air. A solitary tear trickled down my cheek.

I knew the reality of the threat of violence which hung over many women and girls too. I had read about the very real possibility of violence which affected every woman and girl in all areas of her life. It was the fear of that threat of violence which fed the decisions of what to wear before a woman could leave the house. It was the same threat which lay behind the fear of every woman peering over her shoulder as she walked home from school or work searching for a possible threat that lay just beyond the darkness. It was also the same terror which directed the choices women made on where to go and with whom. I had prided myself on knowing how to avoid risky situations with strangers. How had this happened to me! I had made another terrible mistake and the terror had found me.

Terrified and shell shocked from the attack I sat in the backseat sobbing convulsively. He half turned as if to speak to me but, as though changing his mind, he turned back to look at the road. His face was hidden in the shadows of the Toyota. My body screamed in pain as my mind teetered on the edge in an attempt to comprehend what had just happened on the side of the road only moments earlier. I spun in the enveloping darkness that swirled on the fringes of my mind. Death was better than the unbearable memory of the sudden brutality and violence that had erupted destroyed everything alive in me. 'I may as well die', I moaned, my wounded soul bleeding inwardly. 'God let me die!' I wailed, guttural sounds wrenched from the depths of my soul. I tried the car door but it was locked. I started pounding the window with bruised fists! He slammed the brakes and I lurched forward hitting my shoulder into the back of the seat in front of me. Fleetingly I thought the car had crashed! A car accident would bring peace if I could only die I agonised, but there was no traffic on the moonlit road. I slid to the floor of the moving car and wept.

The fragility of my life suddenly dawned on me. After the attack he had seemed almost apologetic, offering to help me to the car but I pushed him away. Morbid thoughts filled my mind as the car sped on the road towards Masvingo. I could be dead, lifeless on the gravel and dry scrub, surrounded by trees under the moonlight but I was alive. I did not feel alive though, not for much longer. I had lost too much, the gushing wound in my soul, life ebbing away. I had nothing to live for. Not after tonight. A few minutes ago all I had been was a girl with a broken heart but any hope in healing was violently crushed under the weight of a predator whose face I could not recognise. My future was stolen from me. The sound of weeping filled the darkened car as another wave of anguish washed over me and more desperate sobs convulsed my bruised body. The lights of Masvingo beckoned in the distance. The dial of the digital clock on the car dashboard glowed ominously in the dark. It was half an hour past midnight.

"Where shall I leave you?" his voice cut through my sobs. I could not tell him where I lived. He would only return to hurt me again. I continued sobbing. He drove to a hotel in the town centre of Masvingo just before 1am. He switched off the engine and told me to get out. Walking ahead, he strode to the reception desk and requested a room.

'Single or double room,' I heard the receptionist asking, casting a furtive glance in my direction as I stood in the shadows of the deserted lobby.

'Single room please' he responded as he pulled out a wad of cash from his wallet and slid it across the desk. 'Room 102' the receptionist handed him a key. He walked back to where I stood and slipped the key in my hand.

'I'll see you tomorrow,' he said before turning away and walking out into the night. Following the signs in the hotel corridors I made my way to room 102. As the door shut softly behind me I slid to the floor and broke down again in a puddle of anguished tears. I clawed at my thighs and arms as I desperately tried to stem the wave of raw pain drowning me. I dug my nails deeper, gouging the tender flesh beneath my hands with long jagged lines across my forearms and thighs as I noticed the holes in my purple dress where the stones had ripped through the fabric. My beautiful dress was ruined! Shuddering I traced the raised angry welts on my skin, drawing blood with my nails. I could not feel the pain of the wounds I made. The pain was deep inside me, at the very core of my broken soul. I looked down at the cuts on my thighs and wailed softly.

A loud knock on the door startled me. Cold fear gripped my heart. Was he back? Was the room a ruse to spend the night with me? I had been such a fool! Had the receptionist given him a key to the hotel room? Panic stricken I scrambled to my feet.

'Shumi open the door! I know you're in there!' The muffled voice through the locked door was vaguely familiar. Then I remembered that I had not told him my name. I peered through the key hole. My cousin Terry stood outside the door. Terry, eight years my senior, was Aunt Jo's eldest son. Quietly I opened the door.

'I saw you just now with that guy at the reception. I saw him pay for your room. I know his type. What I don't understand is why you're with him. What are you doing Shumi?' there was unrestrained anger in his voice and his eyes were filled with questions.

I looked away as more tears slid down my face. He took in my reddened eyes and the jagged tears in the fabric of my dirt streaked purple dress. He stepped in and closed the door. The events of the day – Vusi's betrayal, my broken heart, the violent attack-flooded my mind as the tears fell.

'I'm here Shumi,' he said. 'Talk to me.'

With an effort I forced myself to stop weeping. And then I told him everything. It all came gushing out like a waterfall after the summer rains, but only it was not the rain pouring out but my life ebbing away as I recounted what had happened on that deserted road under the moonlight. My voice breaking, I told him about how in the aftermath of the attack I had feared telling my attacker that I lived on the teacher training college campus where he would be able to find me again and so instead I had ended up in a hotel room well after midnight. I told him everything except that there was a man I loved and that he had broken my heart on the day I was raped. Vusi was the reason for my being in that white Toyota late at night but I could not expose my foolishness in loving a man who had violated my trust. I did not tell Terry about the heart-breaking discovery of Vusi's unforgivable betrayal. I did not tell Terry that I had been desecrated by a predator I did not know because of a man I had foolishly chosen to love. I left Masvingo-young, alive and in love but in less than twenty-four hours I was broken, shattered and hopeless. It does not take more than a moment to lose everything. I had been raped. The word hung in the air like a death sentence. I buried my head in my hands and wept.

Clouds covered the bleak morning sun in the gray sky. A cold draught blew into the room. Terry sat in the chair near the bed while his friend Joseph stood at the window. The sound of morning traffic drifted in through the open window. Terry had hatched the plot to capture my attacker when I had told him how he had said that that he would be back in the morning. Terry brought his powerfully built friend Joseph to be the muscle in the ambush. My head throbbed painfully as we waited in silence. Then I heard a gentle knock at the door. I stood up, the abrupt movement sending searing pain through my bruised body. Terry and Joseph exchanged quick looks as Terry silently motioned for me to respond to the knock. Unsteadily I walked towards the door, my heart beating frantically in my chest. I opened the door and he was standing in the doorway, his bulky frame silhouetted in the light from the electric lamps in the corridor behind him. I faced him and saw him fully for the first time. He had a bulbous nose in a wide planed face that sloped from a receding forehead merging in a prominently jutting chin. He smiled, fleshy lips parted to reveal distinctively large teeth. I retreated into the room, stumbling towards the window as tears clouded my eyes.

'I came to check on you. I was worried after last night,' he said as he stepped into the room. Terry and Joseph moved swiftly at the same time. Terry kicked the door shut while Joseph slammed a fist into the man's mid-section. He crumpled to the floor, groaning loudly. Terry stood over him.

'You will pay for what you did to my cousin!' Terry fumed angrily.

Joseph pulled the man up to his feet and swung his fist. It landed with a loud crack on his jaw. He staggered backwards, yelping in pain as he crashed to the floor. Blood flowed from his nose.

'Stop it! Please stop!' I screamed, sickened at the sight of blood. 'You promised you'd talk to him. You didn't say you'd kill him!'

'He must pay! He ruined you! I'll teach this piece of trash a lesson!' Terry raged as he advanced menacingly on the bleeding man.

Terry's words stung. Ruined! I was ruined. What did that mean? Visions of disintegrating and dilapidated ruins filled my mind's eye. I saw decay and death. What would happen to me now that I was ruined I wondered? I had already been rejected before. Could I ever overcome the shame of my ruined state? Could I ever be loved? I had witnessed how Mama had been rejected because of the violence she had suffered at the hands of a man who had vowed to love and cherish her. I knew how she had struggled for years to find acceptance in a world that judged her mercilessly without compassion for a crime which had been committed against her. Was that to be my fate too? That I would be judged too for the injustice inflicted upon me. The same double standards would be used against me. Terry loved me but it was true, I was ruined and what good would ever come from something that was ruined and dying.

The man on the floor whimpered. 'Please don't kill me.'

'What's your name?' Terry demanded.

'I'm Makoni...Piwai Makoni.' He stammered sitting up, the right side of his face was swollen. 'I'm a member of the City Council.'

My heart plummeted in fear. The City Council was the local government arm concerned with the administrative affairs of the town. He was a politician therefore he was untouchable. Terry's eyes flickered with recognition. 'I know you. I've seen your face in the local paper.'

The man nodded as he wiped his bloody nose.

'You're in the council to look after your constituents and not to abuse them. You think this gives you a licence to attack our sisters?' Terry snarled as Joseph advanced.

'I'm sorry! I'm sorry! It's a terrible mistake. Please I truly am sorry!' he pleaded looking at me.

Repulsed I looked at the cowering pile of human flesh that was curled up on the floor. This was the same man who had brutally attacked me while *my* pleas for mercy fell on deaf ears. An innately feeble man who thrived on the power he usurped from his victims, using their fear as a truss for his cowardice.

'Let him go Terry. Leave it.' I said as I turned away. 'He's not worth it.'

# CHAPTER 15

**M**ama wept when she thought I was not listening. I heard her cry through the thin walls in our home. I felt her anguish as her haunted eyes followed me whenever I walked into the room. She tried to be strong but I could sense she was breaking under the pain of knowing what I had endured and in some way she blamed herself for my trauma. I overheard her tell Aunt Jo when they thought I was asleep. I knew the truth though, that I was to blame. I had fallen in love and that was the reason why I was in this desperate place, hanging between life and death. Love was supposed to bring out the good in people. But naivety, immaturity and unspeakable shame had surfaced instead. I had been a fool and a fool in love is the biggest fool. I had been a fool to believe Vusi and to trust Vusi that he would value my vulnerability and protect it. I had been conceited enough to believe that what we had would last for a lifetime and I had failed myself by walking towards a lie and now there was nothing left but pain, shame and regret.

If only I had not met Vusi. If only I had not travelled to Victoria Falls a day earlier than I had planned on that fateful Thursday morning. *If only*, those words became a prison I could not escape from. My waking moments filled with the curse of regret. One bad decision had changed my life irrevocably. I could not undo the damage of a choice I had made and I could not share the knowledge of what I had done to cause this to happen to me. Mama pleaded to know why I had been in Bulawayo on that evening but I could not tell her that I had been travelling to visit a man who had betrayed me. She could not know about Vusi and what I had done. It would be my grief and shame to carry. I could not bear her judgement twice over. The revelation of who I truly was would crush me all over again. So when she asked I would turn away and hold on to the silence as it unfurled in the distance between us. I concealed my pain when conversation died as I entered a room. I carefully masked my grief when furtive glances were cast in my direction when I passed and when I returned to college I suppressed the urge to run when a white Toyota sedan drove past me. I carried the silence everywhere and intertwined with my pain it became a part of who I was.

Piwai Makoni was too powerful to prosecute and Terry agreed that it would be futile to try. Mama did not press the matter when I refused to press charges. In some ways I think she was relieved. The truth was the shame I carried was far heavier and more pressing than my need for justice. I knew that court proceedings meant I would relive the ordeal over again. The shame was never too far, crippling me with feelings of worthlessness with each passing day. The shame would be made public. I had already noticed the stares and heard the rumours. Terry had insensitively quizzed me about the nature of my relationship with Piwai Makoni weeks after the attack. He pleaded with me to tell him the truth. Even though it crushed my heart to listen to the doubt in his voice when I was suffering under the burden of my pain I understood why he doubted me and I could not blame him.

Piwai Makoni paid for my hotel room and he had returned to the same hotel room the following morning. The question on everyone's mind was why he had done that after he attacked me. They wondered if at all what I accused him of was what had truly happened. It was unusual for a predator to be so generous they left unsaid. I did not have the answers, only questions. What could be unnatural in his behaviour in paying for my hotel room when he had forcibly taken my freedom and stripped me of my soul, especially if it served him to discredit me? Or perhaps somewhere in his demented mind he thought the assault was the unfolding of a relationship spawned out of his violent attack. I did not know what normal predator behaviour was or if a predator could even be normal. I saw his feeble gesture to provide shelter after he attacked me as nothing more than guilt on his part. I knew however that in the event of a trial I few would believe me, an impressionable girl with questionable morals standing up to a powerful public figure in the community. The battle was heavily rigged against me simply because I was a woman.

Vusi called every night after supper. I did not go to the phone booth. When they called my name in the corridors to come to the phone I pretended I was not in my room. I kept the door locked so when they knocked there was complete silence. I would lie on the bed, tears running down my face as I contemplated what to do to make him stop calling. Vusi belonged in a time and place that I could never hope to be a part of anymore. What was that phrase I had overheard the neighbours say about me when they did not realise their whispers carried in the wind? *"Damaged goods"*. They had said I was damaged goods and Vusi would never want me back if he knew what had happened to me. He would never call again if he knew the truth. I was not worth fighting for. I had nothing to forgive. It did not matter that he betrayed me and that I had caught him in the very act. He would be right to walk away from me now and stop calling. Terry was right that night in the hotel when he said that I was ruined.

As the days became weeks the pain held my heart in a vice like grip. I struggled to breathe when my mind was assailed with the memories of that terrifying moonlit night. The triggers to my pain were often innocuous sights, objects or sounds. I would hear the wind rustling through tree branches at night when sleep eluded me and panic stricken I would curl up in a ball on my bed and weep into my pillow. Sometimes I would see the moon from my window on a moonlit night and my body would seize up in spasms that left me drained and weak. Some days I would see dry scrub on the side of a gravel road and my chest would tighten in fear and I would stifle a scream. I knew they whispered about me and I endured the knowing looks and pointing fingers but I kept my anguish hidden because I would not let the world see my brokenness. I would not unravel because of the pain, because they expected me to. I would prevail just as I had so many times before.

Five weeks after the attack, everything unravelled and my world crashed down around me just as I was beginning to come to terms with what had happened to me. It had been a particularly bad week as I had just started on semester exams. Studying long hours into the night had left me feeling tired and sleep deprived. Then a bout of flu had worsened the fatigue and I was battle worn, struggling with nausea and dehydration. I decided to visit the Campus Clinic for flu medication. During the consultation the Clinic nurse asked if I had other complaints besides the flu and I remembered the sharp pain in my pelvis I had felt during my monthly cycle just three weeks before. My monthly cycle had also been uncharacteristically spotty and light. I was unprepared for her next question. She asked if I'd had unprotected intercourse. Six weeks earlier and I would have smiled shyly and giggled while shaking my head. Six weeks earlier and I would have responded with an empathic no. Instead the bile rose in my throat and my body trembled. She looked at me quizzically as I struggled to compose myself. Fleetingly I thought I would tell her of the rape. It would help explain my reaction. She was a nurse after all and she could help. Just as quickly as the thought came I shut it down as I remembered that it would mean one more person would know of my shame. Some wounds would never heal.

"No I have not been with a man recently", I said numbly.

"Pee in that cup and leave it on the shelf in the bathroom" she responded as she passed a specimen jar towards me. She pointed me towards the bathroom door in the brightly lit corridor opposite the consultation room. Ten minutes later she called me back into the consultation room.

"The test I ran on your urine reveals the likelihood of a urinary tract infection which will have to be confirmed with more tests. However, I also took the liberty of running another test just to make sure that whatever drug is prescribed for use is safe in your state. I assume you already know that you're pregnant"

PREGNANT!!! NO!! I recoiled in horror as the unimaginable truth dawned on me that somehow my body had betrayed me and managed to conceive a child in circumstances shrouded in betrayal, grief, loss, terror and shame. I lay awake in my bed many nights after I received the news of my pregnancy. A life was growing inside of my body. I was angry and confused! How was it possible that I was carrying a child! Why would God allow such a thing while I was still broken and raw from what had happened to me? Why was this happening to me! I wept and begged God to take the baby out of my womb. I could not be a mother to a child I had not asked for or wanted. I was only a child myself! I was just nineteen years! I screamed inwardly at the thought of my dreams and aspirations destroyed forever. Mama would never forgive me and she would never accept my child. My friends would leave me. I was completely alone in the world. I wept bitterly as I railed against a world that had conspired to crush my dreams and destroy my life. My whole life was a pile of burning ashes, all my hopes and plans razed to the ground in one word. PREGNANT!

As the days slid by I agonised over the unseen life growing in my belly. It was a life not borne out of love or fidelity but it was a life nevertheless and that life deserved a chance. Growing up it had been imbued in my soul that the life I breathed was God's mercy and will and that the DNA I carried was His blueprint for who He was in me. This child carried the same DNA. I did not have the power to create life; neither did I have the power to terminate it. The sanctity of the new life growing in my body trumped my own pain and personal trauma. I would have to do everything possible to protect this child. I could not let my child grow in the shadow of the same rejection I had struggled with all my life. This was my child. The realisation that this was my child too filled me with hope as I grappled with questions about my future. I would find a way because somehow I was going to raise a child on my own. The road ahead was filled with uncertainty.

> 'I DID NOT HAVE THE POWER TO CREATE LIFE; NEITHER DID I HAVE THE POWER TO TERMINATE IT THE SANCTITY OF THE NEW LIFE GROWING IN MY BODY TRUMPED MY OWN PAIN AND PERSONAL TRAUMA.

Three weeks later I made a trip into town to buy a few school supplies. It was a dreary Saturday morning with a cold, blustery wind that sounded like mournful moaning as it blew through the trees. Wind swept leaves floated in muddy puddles on the path leading to the hostel as I made my way back to my room. I was eager to strip off my wet socks and shoes and slip into bed for some much needed warmth. As I drew closer I could make out a figure huddling in the entrance hallway in a black knit sweater and blue denim jeans. There was something familiar about the build of his broad shoulders and tall frame. His head turned at the sound of my approaching footsteps. I caught my breath and froze, silence filling the deserted hallway. Vusi stood two feet away from me.

His face was drawn, dark circles under his eyes. He looked older and tired. He opened his mouth to speak and as if deciding against it, he sighed heavily as he looked at me. I broke the silence.

"What are you doing here?" My voice sounded strange, strained and shallow, as though it was not my own.

He stepped towards me warily. "Can we go and talk? Somewhere private?" he asked. His voice was taut with tension. Numb with the shock of seeing him standing so close I closed my eyes and opened them again. I was not imagining his presence in the hallway. He was still standing in front of me. Suddenly I felt the plastic handles of the shopping bags cutting into the flesh of my hands. I needed to put down the packages I was carrying but not here in the hallway. I turned towards the corridor which led to the room I shared with my friend Esther. Vusi followed silently.

He sat on the edge of my bed nervously watching me as I unpacked the shopping bags and neatly organised my supplies into my cupboard. When I was done I sat on Esther's bed facing him and quietly folded my freezing hands in my lap. His voice filled the room.

"Shumi I'm sorry. I messed everything up. I was selfish and stupid and I hurt you! I know I can't ask you to forgive me. I don't have a right to ask that of you but all I am asking for is that you would give me a chance to prove to you that I will do better. I can do better. I promise I will do it right this time. Please Shumi just another chance." His voice trailed off as he looked away, his eyes glistening with tears.

"I can't be with you Vusi. Everything has changed now. Too much has happened. We are over. We can't ever be. You came here for nothing. Just leave" My voice broke as tears filled my eyes.

I could not tell him about the rape. He would reject me too as so many had done before. There was no hope left for us now, not after the rape. It would be my silent torment and unspoken shame. Seeing him had only rekindled the flame I still carried in my heart for him. I did not understand why he had fractured our love with his selfishness but I knew that I would have found a way to forgive him if he had asked for my forgiveness earnestly enough but now it was too late.

"I know Shumi" he said softly. He stood up and walked to where I sat. Kneeling in front of me he clasped my hands in his. His hands were warm and soft, like a winter fire infusing life into my cold skin. I tried to pull away but he held mine tightly. My heart ached at what was once familiar and safe but I could never have that in my life again; not with him. I closed my eyes as the tears slid down my face.

"Shumi look at me."

I shook my head. "No you don't know Vusi! You don't know anything!" I cried desperately pulling away.

"I know about the rape...." His voice choked as he struggled to compose himself. He stroked my hands gently as he continued. "It changes nothing. I still love you".

I froze at the realisation that somehow Vusi knew. He knew that I had been raped. The word hung in the air like a dark and heavy cloud casting its ugly shadow in the room. I pulled away, anger and pain surging in my mind as I recoiled at the realisation that Vusi knew my shame. The question rushing in my head, how did he know! Esther! She must have been the one who had told him! Angry tears tumbled down my face. I was aghast at her betrayal and how could she have done such a thing especially when I had never spoken to her about what had happened to me. I knew she had heard the rumours. She had tried to ask me but it was not her story to tell. It was my anguish and my painful shame. She had no right to speak about it especially to Vusi. It was too late. Vusi knew and I felt ashamed and dirty again.

"I'm sorry Shumi. I'm sorry this happened to you. It's my fault. I put you in harm's way." He pulled me closer as he continued. "I can't make it go away. I can't undo it. But I can work at making you happy for the rest of my life. I love you. I always will. I want to be with you. Nothing changes the way I feel about you Shumi!"

I was sobbing now, the all too familiar waves of pain ripping through my mind. It's too late I thought! I had longed for Vusi to come and tell me that he was sorry the day I walked out of his home in Victoria Falls and even then I would have forgiven him. I would have put my arms around him leaning on his strong chest as I listened to the rhythm of his beating heart and his arms would have held me too while I cried at the thought of his betrayal but it was too late now. I was pregnant. I was carrying another man's child. His eyes widened in shock as he pulled back to look at me. Shaking I realised that I must have said it out loud in my grief stricken state. Now Vusi knew that I was pregnant!

"It's not your baby!" I sobbed. "It's not your baby!" The sobs wracked my body as I slumped onto the bed and wept, defeated and heartbroken. Vusi had taken precautions on that first night together. He knew the truth just as I did that the consummation of our love did not result in conception. He knew the child I was carrying could not be his even though it had been my frantic hope that he was the father. I desperately wished I was carrying Vusi's baby because then it would have made sense to be with him right now in spite of all that had happened to me. But it was not Vusi's baby. His arms encircled my heaving shoulders as he lifted my face up to his.

"I'll marry you Shumi. Nobody has to know about this. You haven't told anybody yet have you?" His eyes searched mine as I sat up confused. He stood up and sat on the bed next to me. "This baby will be ours Shumi. It's your baby and therefore mine. Biology be damned! It will not stand in the way of what I feel for you and the child you're carrying." He held me close as we both wept.

I spent the rest of the day in an emotion filled daze as he spoke about how we would have to inform my family of my condition and that he was the one responsible. He made me swear to never breathe a word of the true parentage of my child. He warned me of the stigma which would be attached to our family if it was ever revealed that conception had been in the aftermath of the rape. I could hardly believe that everything had changed so quickly and dramatically. He was here, sitting next to me. His brown eyes though deepened with recent pain reflected hope and renewed confidence. His arms tightened around me and I felt safe again. I was back in his secure embrace and it felt like home.

The ensuing weeks were filled with busy plans for our traditional wedding ceremony. Vusi was expected to converge at our home with a delegation comprising of his family members in order to pay the *roora* which was the dowry given to my family in exchange for my hand in marriage. I saw the relief in my mother's eyes when I informed her that I had a boyfriend and that he wanted to marry me. She had smiled through her tears as she whispered a quick prayer. That I was pregnant was a double blessing. The heavens had smiled upon her at last and I was freed from the shame of being 'damaged goods' and 'ruined'. If she ever wondered at the paternity of my pregnancy she did not voice her secret musings on the subject. Elated, she consulted with her relatives on the arrangements to be made for the ceremony. An emissary was sent to my father's family in Marondera to invite them to the proceedings and a date was set. It was to take place in the springtime in September when the Jacaranda trees were in full bloom.

The ceremony was a simple and understated affair. Aunt Jo managed the catering with the help of my cousins. Vusi and his delegation were received at the gate by my uncle Francis who had travelled from Masvingo to be in attendance at my marriage ceremony. "You're a beautiful bride" my husband whispered when the ceremony was over and my in-laws introduced and welcomed. Husband! The word held so much safety and comfort. My mind whirled with a myriad of emotions; gratitude, happiness and unbridled excitement! My joy was complete because finally I found where I belonged. I was married to my best friend, Vusi and I were one now, and the future was filled with the promise of more love and hope. I was beginning to feel whole again, my pain subsiding into healing and restoration.

We were sublimely happy as a married couple. Vusi treated me with kindness and consideration. I shuttled between Masvingo and Victoria Falls till I became too heavy to travel and my delivery date drew close. The arrival of my beautiful son several months after we were married sealed our joy. He looked just like me with smooth ebony skin and dimpled cheeks. Vusi named him Thamsanqa which means blessing. Vusi was gentle and patient as I stumbled through my new role as a mother and wife. He had a way with Thami as he fondly called our son. Vusi was everything I had always dreamt fatherhood should be; available, intentional and loving. As the weeks turned into months I settled into a comfortable transition of living with the man who had become my greatest blessing and my son-an unexpected love and true gift from a dark place in my life. I had never been happier.

# CHAPTER 16

As with every new relationship between two people after a while it settles into a comfortable place of familiarity and routine. I did not notice when the subtle shift in our relationship occurred. I had a new job at the local school and the busy days occupied my days so fully that at first I missed the tension and growing emotional distance between Vusi and I. He still played with Thami. Thami was an energetic, curious 3-year-old toddler who frequently tore through the house kicking his soccer ball into furniture much to my annoyance. Vusi would leap to his defence and bundle Thami outside while reminding me not to stand in the way of greatness because according to him Thami was a budding soccer champion. They would kick the ball outside until the sun dipped out of view and the shadows blended into the darkening sky. It was not long before Vusi started coming home late from work. Thami would plaster his face against the window, watchfully peering into the gathering darkness for Vusi's return. I would peel him away from his post and prepare him for bed after supper amidst tears and screams. Vusi offered few explanations for his late nights beyond the terse statement that he was 'at work'. I also knew they had seasonal periods of busy days that slipped into nights particularly at the end of the month. I did not mind Vusi having an occasional late night out with his friends as long as he communicated that he would be late. Vusi's late nights however were no longer occasional or seasonal and he did not explain why. He came in late every day of the week and soon even during the weekends he was no longer available to spend time with me and Thami.

I knew something was wrong but I could not confront Vusi over the issue except to occasionally ask him why he was spending another weekend away. He became sullen when I showed interest in his plans or activities and so I retreated and stopped asking questions. We barely spoke. He was distant and cold when he was home although Thami was the only one who received a warm acknowledgement. Rationalising that this was a passing phase I quietly ignored his late nights and lengthy absences from home. He was free to come and go as he pleased without question as long as he was coming home. I immersed myself in my work and domestic responsibilities turning a blind eye to the growing discordance between us. I desperately hoped that the crisis he was going through would end. Foolishly l also believed that if I paid no attention to it, then eventually he would work his way through the issues that had caused him to drift away from us and he would find his way back to us.

The longer he stayed away, the deeper I buried the painful truth about the crisis in my marriage, unwilling to face the devastation it was causing me. I just needed more faith I reasoned, avoiding the painful realisation that I was married to a man who had become a stranger. Vusi no longer veiled the venom in his words, frequently calling me stupid and ugly when he lost his temper. I held onto the cloak of silence as a form of protection. I was not naïve; I knew that there was another unseen shadow in our marriage, most likely another woman. I was not ready to put a name to the threat that lurked in the darkness which was destroying my marriage. As long as she remained nameless I could pretend that she did not exist. I grew more silent as our marriage turned cold and the distance stretched out wider between us.

I was not the first young wife to deal with infidelity. I had experienced the trauma of infidelity before, in our young relationship when I had discovered his betrayal and soon after that my trauma had been compounded by the devastation of the rape. Our reconciliation and subsequent marriage just a few weeks later was overshadowed by the need for secrecy to protect my child. Vusi's acceptance of my pregnant condition had veiled the damaging impact of his infraction. We had never spoken about it again and yet I still carried the wreckage of the trauma of his betrayal. The recurrence of his infidelity less than five years into our marriage plunged me deep into the darkness of my trauma again. I struggled with the malignancy of the poison in our marriage, the raw pain and wounds he was inflicting on me and yet the effects of his infidelity were quickly dismissed in conversations with other women.

"You'll get over it."

"All men do it."

"Be strong."

I did not understand how I was expected to live in anticipation that my heart would one day be broken and when the devastating pain came I was the one who inexplicably felt ashamed and guilty. I did not know how to be strong when I lived in constant fear of his rejection. In the end I only felt more wounded by the fact that I had to hide my pain. The scars were imprinted indelibly upon my mind. I struggled to sleep and when I did sleep I was haunted by nightmares I could not escape from. Assailed with debilitating self-doubt and struggling with insomnia-I began eating poorly and became overly anxious. I had always feared rejection but it was no longer a fear I harboured for myself. There was someone else in our lives to consider now, my son Thami.

I knew what Vusi was capable of because I had seen the damage and experienced the bitterness of his betrayal. I was not blinded to his flaws and yet I had missed the lesson in his deception; that he could hurt me again. In my haste to find comfort and to belong I had walked back into his arms where I was vulnerable to the wounds he would inflict. I thought he loved me and I was desperate to believe that he did. I had not questioned his actions and in so doing I had missed the signs that it perhaps it was not love that had brought him back to me but driven by guilt at what had happened to me he had found a way to make amends by marrying me. I was imprisoned in a loveless relationship because the reason that brought us together was practical and right, based on an emotion so powerful that it felt and looked like love. Guilt could never be love but it could justify something that felt so right.

As I grew more silent, he became more hurtful and cruel. The silence became my unspoken resistance to his late night absences, a passive-aggressive reaction to his cruelty and insensitive attempts to provoke me whenever he stumbled into the house drunk and verbally abusive. Vusi was as intelligent as he was both stubborn and proud and he would brook no resistance from me, spoken or unspoken. He regarded the silence as insolence and he only became more hurtful in retaliation. His speech became vile towards me until finally one morning the silence snapped.

Vusi had returned home in the early hours of morning reeking of the cheap home distilled wine from the local tavern and even cheaper perfume. He made his way to the bed in the darkened bedroom noisily tripping over furniture. He pulled the blanket off my body as he rolled next to me with a loud thud. A few seconds later our bedroom filled with his loud snores. I checked the time on the clock which was on the bedside table. The luminous dials glowed in the dark-4AM. I could not sleep so I got up and left the bedroom deciding that my chores would begin early that day. I swept and cleaned the house while making preparations for breakfast. Thami was still asleep and would be up at 7AM. The early morning sun rays peeked behind the drawn curtains casting a golden glow in the bedroom when I walked in three hours later. Vusi's shoes were still on his feet as he slept fully clothed in the bed. My bottles of body creams and other toiletries were strewn on the floor from earlier when he had stumbled in the dark. Humming quietly, I picked them up as Vusi stirred on the bed. His bloodshot eyes were fixed on me as I continued folding clothes.

"Quiet!" he growled from the bed. "You're giving me a headache!"

"You did that entirely on your own" I muttered softly beneath my breath as I pulled back the curtains. Bright light flooded the room.

Vusi winced in the sudden light as he sat up, the tension thick in his voice. "Did you say something?"

"Did you hear something?" I retorted as I turned away.

His arm shot up and caught me on the small of my back. I staggered forward from the sheer force of his blow and crashed into the vanity bureau, scattering the bottles of toiletries on the floor. Stunned by the suddenness of the assault I whimpered in pain as I saw a gash across my arm where a bottle had cut me. Memories of my mother bleeding from my father's vicious beatings flashed through my mind and a swell of emotions rose. I would not be a victim! I would never permit a man to raise his hand against me without standing up for myself! Enraged I pushed myself up and hurled my body to where he stood with all the strength I could muster. He toppled backwards and slammed into the wall behind him, his head making a loud cracking sound as he made contact. Grunting he slid to the floor. I ran from the room as he stood up, glowering with rage. He caught me just as I reached the kitchen and pummelling me with his right hand he pinned me down with his left elbow. I kicked out wildly as his blows rained down on me. Blackness threatened to overcome me as his punches became more vicious. Screaming I kicked out again and this time caught him in the groin. He doubled over, clutching frantically between his legs. I kicked him again, this time harder and he fell to the floor, wailing in pain. I staggered to my feet and stood over him and kicked him over and over again while he lay writhing in pain on the floor. Then I saw Thami standing in the kitchen doorway, tears quietly streaming down his face. He was watching us in horror just as I had done many years ago when my father attacked my mother. I slumped against the wall with my head in my hands and started weeping uncontrollably.

Our lives descended into a cycle of protracted violence. Vusi would perceive my reaction as provocative and he would unleash a new wave of violent beatings and I would hit back, which infuriated him and only served to enrage him further. The violence filled our days and Thami was caught up as a witness to the dysfunction spiralling out of control in our home. Vusi began to stay away from home for extended periods of time when he realised that I would not hesitate to fight back despite the blackened eyes and swollen lips I had after each bruising encounter. He bore the scars of my rage too; bite marks on his arms and long jagged scratches on his face. My heart grew colder the longer he stayed away. Late nights turned into early mornings and soon he was spending days away from home.

I spent days festering in loneliness and anger while his absences caused me great frustration even if I restrained myself and did not vocalise my true feelings. When he was home everything I did and said in my heightened emotional state was provocation; a carelessly spoken word would push him over the edge and he would explode into rage. Seeking an outlet for my own pent up emotions, I met his rage, blow for blow until it would dissipate in tears and blood as our bruised bodies retreated from the fight. I was terrified and overwhelmed but I was also angry to bursting point. I wanted to inflict on his flesh the pain he caused deep in my wounded soul. Seeing the cuts, I had made on his face or the bruises on his body I would feel a small sense of triumph but I knew that there were no winners in this war. We were losing and so was our son.

Then I met Sylvia. She worked at the local grocery store and she always had a welcoming smile every time I saw her. On one of my trips to the store she invited me to church. It had been three years since I had been to a church service. In the aftermath of the rape I had shuttered my heart to religion and matters of faith. I had a multitude of questions but there were no answers. Why had God permitted the rape? I loved my son but why had my son been the result of a violent conception? Was I being punished? The questions had swirled in my head until one afternoon three months before I delivered my son, engulfed in pain, I had resolved to never set foot in a church again.

My marriage was failing and I was struggling with anxiety and the physical loneliness that accompanied our loveless union. What harm could possibly come out of going back to the one place that had always been my source of strength? I decided to visit Sylvia's church the following Sunday. It was a small vibrant church of the Pentecostal faith that was located a short walking distance away from home. I sat in the middle row on the backless bench in the dimly lit church building. Sunlight streamed through the huge windows at the front of the building, where a motley of well-worn music instruments and a chipped wooden pulpit were placed on a raised platform that served as a podium. Chairs were lined up in neat rows at the front where the choir sat. The rest of the church building was filled with wooden benches running the length of the room.

The service programme began with impassioned pleas for

repentance and rapturous prayer. I sat motionless on the unforgiving wooden bench, steeling myself against the familiar stirrings in my heart to whisper a prayer or sing a verse of praise in response. The building filled with voices praying in unison. I began to tremble as sobs engulfed my body as I wept. The floodgates of the pain I had suppressed in my grieving heart for a long time crashed wide open and reliving the trauma of my rape years ago I shuddered as the tears flowed. My body heaved as the fear, pain and shame rose to the surface and my chest tightened as emotion overcame me. The praying voices reached a crescendo and the tightening in my chest yielded, giving way to a stillness which settled over me. Eventually the tears subsided and I opened my eyes as song filled the small church.

I began attending Sunday service with Thami. I would wake up early on Sunday mornings and prepare for service just like Mama had taken us to church with her every Sunday. I had come full circle and I was home. The world was full of pain and trauma and I had no control over the shadows which lurked in the world ready to strike and inflict pain. I just needed to find a safe place to heal; a place where I could be reminded to live in complete faith, trusting in the hand of a God who would never leave me. I knew now that God had never left me. I had turned my back on Him when my world had been ripped apart. My trust had been violated and my spirit crushed under the unbearable assault of violence, infidelity and trauma. This was the ugliness that was inevitably a part of the world I lived in and I could not control that. The only power I had was in choosing to believe in myself and the power of all I could still be. I had to trust my convictions-in who I was and not in my circumstances or the events that I had experienced. I could not change my past or rewrite my history but I could create my present and my future. The challenges and struggles I faced were temporary but my destiny and purpose were eternal.

Led by a fairly young and gifted charismatic leader who displayed great skill in preaching and interpretation of the Scriptures I soon became a regular attendee of both the Sunday morning and mid-week evening services. As the preacher thundered on the pulpit my faith rose, buoyed by the testimonies of my spiritual leader and his faithful flock. If desperate circumstances could be turned around in the lives of those who shared their stories of triumph in church Sunday after Sunday, then my failing marriage could easily be restored if I pressed on and did not waver in faith. Vusi did not change even though I prayed and spent long hours in the study of the Bible. He remained cold and distant and there was no miraculous shift in our marriage. If I expected a miracle I was quickly disillusioned of that hope. Vusi had free will and I could not rush him into changing. His will remained and I could not manipulate him into subverting his will for mine-no matter how well-meaning my intentions were. Vusi would have to find his own way to his redemption.

I discovered I was pregnant three months, the result of one unex-pected night when Vusi had come home early. Discovering that I was pregnant was both unsettling and terrifying. I agonised on how Vusi would receive the news. I had wistfully believed that he would start coming home early after that night but the hours had only grown longer as he continued to stay away. I was terrified that the news of my pregnancy would be the final straw for our marriage. Surprisingly, Vusi was happy, smiling exuberantly when I told him that he was to be a father. It was my second pregnancy and his first biological child. Vusi had shown nothing but great love for Thami but we both knew the truth, that he was not Thami's biological father. He had provided Thami with a home and even given him his name. He regarded Thami as his own, staying true to his promise that he would love Thami as his son, but he was also a man yearning for his own progeny and finally I was carrying his child, a blessing and precious gift which provided a reprieve to the crisis in our marriage.

Our home became peaceful and happy again. Vusi stopped coming home late at night and weekends were spent at home with our son and my growing belly. He rubbed my feet, cooked and cleaned when I was too tired to do anything. I was happy and grateful, thankful for the love in our home again. Everything was as it should be and my life was finally alright. The tranquillity of the peace in our home flourished as our newly revived love blossomed. He still would not go to church with me and so a part of me was terrified at the fragility of our renewed peace. "Would it last?" I brooded. Nevertheless, I embraced the uncertainty of our rekindled love and immersed myself in the beauty of being cherished and loved again. I had what I had prayed for; I had the gift of a husband who loved me in the present and that was all I needed. I would embrace all of it while I yet had the time. Vusi was mine.

Our son, Nkosilathi *(God with us)* was born in May. It was autumn in Victoria Falls and the trees outside our house were bare, shedding their leaves as the cold settled in. Vusi was excited at the arrival of our son Nkosi as we affectionately loved to call him. He spent the first three months of Nkosi's life carrying him in his arms whenever he was home and Nkosi would fall asleep in his arms as he watched soccer on Saturday afternoons on the television in the living room. I would walk in to see Vusi dozing off in front of the television with little Nkosi on his chest and It was a beautiful sight to see; father and son asleep peacefully in our home.

The peace did not last however as Nkosi was a fussy child. I could not pacify Nkosi when he would wake up and fill the nights with his colicky wailing. Thami was an active and energetic 4-year-old by then while Nkosi needed my full attention. I was overwhelmed and soon

Vusi began to find fault with me. Our home was not as neat as he would have liked it to be and perhaps it was the taxing routine of our busy household with two young children and a young sleep deprived wife which ended our happy family reverie. By the time the blustery winds of August started blowing, Vusi was coming home late again. Winter was ending but a cold season of loneliness entered our home. My brief dance with joy was over.

# CHAPTER 17

The 90's were characterised by social and economic turmoil in Zimbabwe. The 1992 drought had drastically reduced agricultural output which was the mainstay of the economy. As the country emerged from the devastating effects of the drought there were other challenges to be faced as many local firms began to struggle due to trade barriers with neighbouring countries and increased competition in the region. The position of Zimbabwe which had once been an economic powerhouse in the region weakened and by the turn of the century in 2000, unemployment rose, inflation spiralled upwards and the quality of life fell. Vusi and I had to evaluate the cost of continuing to live in Zimbabwe in the midst of a declining economy. The future of our young family was at stake.

Neighbouring South Africa was now under the leadership of the African National Congress with President Thabo Mbeki at the helm. The economic performance of the country was on the rise since the advent of democracy in 1994. South Africa's currency was holding steady against the major currencies in the world while the country was on a massive construction drive with world class infrastructure development. Jobs were available in the burgeoning economy. South Africa became a very attractive option for Vusi and I. We were both educated and skilled workers and willing to work hard to build a future for our family. In 2002 we decided to relocate to South Africa.

I sat across Pastor Nkiwane in a small brightly lit office at the

Jesus Reigns Ministries in Johannesburg. Vusi and I were now living in South Africa. Vusi had been the first to join the trek of thousands of hopefuls to cross the Limpopo River to seek better opportunities in South Africa in the previous year. I had joined him six months later in the town of Ermelo when he found a job in the eastern province of Mpumalanga. The harsh reality of navigating a foreign country with two young children while seeking employment had pushed me to make the decision to leave Thami and Nkosi in the care of my mother in Zimbabwe. It had been a very difficult decision to make especially since they were still very young. Thami was now enrolled in the elementary class at the local primary school and Nkosi was just over 2 years old.

I searched for a job but Ermelo held no fruitful prospects for me. Vusi did not hide his displeasure at my lack of success in securing a job. Often he would suggest that it would be better if I returned to Zimbabwe to care for our children where I would be more useful. His resentment at my continued presence only grew with each unsuccessful attempt to get employment. He hardly spoke to me, only grunting in response when I greeted him at the end of his working day. I felt the seething rage behind his quiet demeanour. It was the all too familiar tension-filled lull before the storm erupted. I knew that if I stayed, then the violence was inevitable. Resentment was brewing and I had to escape before it exploded.

A week later I was in Johannesburg as Pastor Nkiwane perused through the document in his hands. It was my resume. My long time best friend from primary school, Judith, was now living and working in South Africa. She was a consultant with a recruitment firm in Pretoria. She had invited me to visit her for a while. Relieved I had jumped at the reprieve the visit offered me from Vusi's simmering rage in Ermelo. During my visit I had shared with her my growing desperation at my unemployed status. Females were less likely to be hired for jobs men were also qualified for she had surmised. The options available to me were in the hospitality industry as a waitress or cleaner. My shoulders sagged. I had heard the horror stories of long thankless nights in the hotel industry with some restaurants exploiting desperate job seekers by not offering a salary base. Sadly, some restaurant employees were working solely for customer generated tips.

"What else can you do besides teaching Shumi?" Judith persisted.

"I've got a certificate in Bible Study from my church back home." My voice trailed off as I hung my head in shame.

Her eyes lit up. "Now that can work!" she exclaimed. "Women are perfect in ministry. I know how passionate you are about women and children. You are kind, compassionate and nurturing. Those are compelling qualities in ministry. With your teaching experience you'd be an amazing minister!" She smiled as she continued, amused at my obvious confusion.

"Ministry work is real work Shumi. It's challenging because it is about leadership and moral responsibility but it is also about integrity and relationship building. People are struggling with issues and they need love and compassion. It's like being a spiritual psychologist to people who need your support and guidance."

Bewildered I looked at her. What was she saying!

"You're going into pastoral work Shumi! And I know just the person to guide you!"

I remembered when I was 10 and I made the decision to become a nun. Life had dealt me a different hand and I was married now with two children. The dreams of a ten-year-old girl were a distant memory of what was once possible in another lifetime. Yet in an inexplicable twist of events I was once again contemplating serving humanity in the same way, just a different title. Purpose and providence had found me again. It was true that I was passionate about empowering women and that I loved children. Intertwining that with a deep seated desire to serve would make it my life's call. I was intrigued.

And so here I was sitting in a chair in Pastor Nkiwane's office as he continued to attentively go through my resume. After a short while he lifted his head and began to speak.

"Your resume is good but it focuses more on your teaching experience in the secular system of education. Your focus will have to make the shift to education from a Christian perspective. You will need to emphasize what you can contribute towards the development of a Christian centred education system."

I nodded my head as he continued speaking.

Pastor Nkiwane was a renowned evangelical figure in religious circles in South Africa. He led a congregation of thousands of believers across several branches of well delineated ministry branches which included healing, teaching and counselling. I hoped to become a mentee in the teaching ministry which was flourishing under his leadership. Judith was a prominent member of his rapidly growing church and it was her influence that had yielded this rare meeting with the church leader. His eyes were deep reflective pools of kindness belying an innate intelligence and perceptiveness. He had a gentleness about him as he asked about my marriage and children. Perhaps it was the note of kindness in his voice or the compassion in his eyes that caused the truth to tumble out. Amidst sobs and tears I shared the trauma I had experienced culminating in my fractured relationship with my husband and the breakdown of my marriage 5 years later.

"You've been through quite a lot Mrs Ndlovu and the pain is still quite raw." He surmised perceptively at the end of my account. I was born in a time of war and raised by a violent man. My first child had been conceived out of violence and my marriage marred by abuse at the hands of an unfaithful man. For as long as I could remember my life had embodied shame while I blamed myself for circumstances I had no control over. I blamed myself for the abuse and the violence and had submitted to living a lie because I thought anything was better than facing the harsh truth surrounding my childhood and now my marriage. I was a survivor of violence and yet I had hidden it away from the world because I thought my shame too great to bear but it was never my shame. The shame and the blame for the suffering and indignity I had endured lay squarely in the hands that had perpetrated the same injustice against me.

Like many others who had suffered an injustice and found no help I had found it easier to shoulder the burden and yet my guilt was unfounded and my blame misplaced. I felt a weight fall away from my heaving shoulders as Pastor Nkiwane counselled me. Vusi no longer had a hold over who I was. His last name and the status of being a respectably married woman, both of which I had used as a shield against an unforgiving world while I wallowed in loneliness and pain, was a false sense of security I no longer needed. What I needed was the grace to forgive myself for the mistakes I had made and to learn from my pain so that I would never hurt myself again by choosing a lie instead of choosing myself. I was a human being and a survivor of violence, still worthy of acceptance, love and respect regardless of my social or marital status. I smiled as I wiped the tears from my face with the back of my hand. The pain was raw but I was finally coming out of the darkness.

I became an associate minister in the teaching school of Jesus Reigns Ministries. My days were filled with morning sessions of prayer, Bible study and discussions followed by busy afternoon tutorials. I was busy and had little free time but I was grateful. I was not a salaried minister as I was registered as a senior volunteer but I did receive an allowance which allowed me to cover basic expenses. It was adequate and I could look after myself without begging Vusi for any help. I could also set aside a small amount of money to send home to Mama and my sons at the end of the month if I cut down on lunch and unnecessary travel to visit Vusi in Mpumalanga. Vusi was not consistent in his efforts to provide for our children but whenever he did send money he was very generous. Our children relied heavily on us both to keep providing for them as we continued to work. I missed them terribly but Mama made certain they never lacked for love either.

Mama had softened with age or perhaps the arrival of her grandsons had given her a warm disposition I had not seen in a very long time. The edge in Mama's temperament vanished as her grandsons revealed a surprising depth of love and gentleness. I did not chafe at our interactions even when we did not agree. She laughed more and her voice when I spoke to her was vibrant and lively. I knew my sons were not easy. They were boisterous boys and Mama had raised daughters only. Her older granddaughters, Rose's children were mild mannered and less adventurous but Mama never complained and laughed when I quizzed her. She was happy and thankful and she often remarked that my boys had given her a new lease on life.

Eighteen months after I started ministerial work in Johannesburg I decided to visit Vusi. The visits to Mpumalanga had dwindled to once every three months until I had completely stopped travelling to Ermelo for close to ten months largely due to my busy schedule at the school. Vusi had visited me only once in the entire time I lived in Johannesburg. He was indifferent to my new vocation and he hardly asked about my work on the rare occasions we spoke. He was frequently in Johannesburg though, spending weekends at a friend's house in Germiston. He would neither call nor visit when he was in

Johannesburg, claiming to have been too busy to drive 45 minutes to where I lived.

I arrived in Ermelo just after 2PM. I knew Vusi would still be at work. It was a Wednesday afternoon. I had picked a Wednesday for my visit partly because I expected he would not have plans to stay out till late on a weekday. Besides I had a conference to attend during the weekend and I needed to travel back to Johannesburg by Friday. I still had a key to our home and I was relieved to find that he had not changed the locks. It was a small sparsely furnished apartment designed for an unmarried tenant with a small kitchen leading into a space used as the living room-cum-bedroom. A neatly made bed stood at the far end of the room. The bathroom door was adjacent to the bed facing the entrance into the apartment. The house was neat as I had expected. Vusi had always been particularly neat and tidy. I opened the refrigerator and smiled as I viewed a bag of frozen fish on the top shelf, some things would never change. I set about preparing his favourite fish dish.

Just after 6PM I heard a key turn in the lock. Vusi was home. The door gently swung open as he walked in. I stood in the doorway of the bathroom at the end of the short passage from where he stood with a look of surprise as he took in the simmering pot on the stove and the table laid out for two. He was carrying a bag in his hands. It was a takeaway bag from the Portuguese restaurant in town. Then I noticed movement behind him and a woman came into view, standing next to him. She was tall and fair skinned with wide hips and a voluptuous chest. Her fingers were adorned with colourful well-manicured long nails. I looked down at my calloused hands and suddenly felt inadequate.

"Hello Vusi" I said mustering up all the cheerfulness I could.

His head swivelled in my direction. "What are you doing here?"

he barked as he closed the door and ushered the beautiful woman into the house. Her eyes silently skimmed over my worn dress and misshapen shoes. The red dress she wore accentuated her attention drawing curves and her shapely legs were encased in a pair of expensive looking heeled boots.

"I thought I'd come to see you Vusi. It's been too long"

He strode towards me. "Not long enough Shumi. Why did you not call? You need to leave."

He jerked my arm as he attempted to draw me towards the door. I dug my heels into the wooden floor, resisting his effort.

"Let go of me Vusi" My voice an ominous whisper. He released my arm and an uneasy silence descended in the room.

"I can see you have dinner already Vusi so let me not get in your way." I said tersely turning towards the stove. I switched the stove off and left the pots to cool. I could not stomach the idea of food. My heart was shattered and I could barely process the raw emotional tumult. They sat on the bed quietly talking as they ate their dinner while I sat on one of the hard backed living room chairs with my back turned away from them. An hour later I heard soft sounds drifting from the bed. My stomach churned as the unmistakable sounds filled the small apartment. I was sitting less than five feet away from where they lay. My chest tightened and my breath became ragged and shallow. I thought that I would pass out from the pain and anguish rising in waves. I wanted to flee this scene of intolerable shame but instead I sat motionless on that unforgiving chair while their bodies shuddered. I could not cry, the well of my tears for Vusi had finally run dry and so I sat on the hard chair until their quietly sleeping bodies breathed softly into the night. I was numb from the unending cycle of humiliation and rejection. I remembered that I still had a choice. I sat on the chair as the thoughts tumbled wildly in my mind that even in this degrading abasement I was worthy; I was a loving mother, a good daughter, a loyal friend, a compassionate teacher, a kind minister. On and on throughout the night I reminded myself of the goodness I had and when the morning sun cast its soft yellow glow into the room as it rose in the sky, I was still sitting on that chair, holding onto it tightly with whitened knuckles. I had survived the night just like I had survived all the other things I thought I would never survive.

Their bodies stirred as they turned in their sleep. I picked up my bag from the floor and closed the door behind me. I had known for a long time that our marriage was over but I was completely blind-sided by Vusi's cruelty and inhumane treatment. The painful horror of the previous night weighed heavily on my mind as I stepped into the growing sunlight. I had known of his infidelity but I had never openly acknowledged the women he entertained in his shameful conduct. I had reasoned that as long as I had no knowledge of who the other women were, I could still leave room in my heart to forgive him. I had accommodated his selfishness and disrespect and even forgiven his indiscretions without receiving a single apology. Unwittingly my passive choice to remain blind while he continued to flagrantly display his disrespect had wounded me deeply, leading to more grief and torment. I could barely recognise who he had become.

As I walked away from the horror of his depravity and heartlessness I knew that this was the end of a painful chapter in my life I would no longer permit Vusi to wound me. I was a single parent now. The realisation filled me with unease and fear but I had no time to feel sorry for myself. I had work to do and I needed to focus while looking after myself and my children. Any hope I

> AS I WALKED AWAY FROM THE HORROR OF HIS DEPRAVITY AND HEARTLESSNESS I KNEW THAT THIS WAS THE END OF A PAINFUL CHAPTER IN MY LIFE I WOULD NO LONGER PERMIT VUSI TO WOUND ME.

held to salvage my marriage of eight years from complete destruction had been dispelled in one night. As I walked through the deserted streets of Ermelo I left behind the man who would now be just another shadow in my past. I had been through pain in most of my twenty-eight years of life but this was not how my story would end. I still had a future and a full life to live and I had every intention to live it well. There is no better way than love I reminded myself. 'Love yourself Shumi' I whispered my voice carrying in the crisp morning air. Love always wins. I was going to win. My life may not have reflected that yet but I knew that love was everything I needed. I quickened my step and as I turned the corner I saw a taxi across the street filling up with passengers. There was room for one more. Soon I was on my way back to Johannesburg as the sun blazed across the cloudless morning sky. I was going to be alright.

# CHAPTER 18

I threw myself into my work relentlessly and became fully occupied with the demands of ministry work. The role I took on became increasingly demanding as the responsibilities shifted allowing me to handle more complex matters. I was completely devoted to the students I tutored and to the ever widening circle of people I ministered to. I met many broken women during my tenure at Jesus Reigns Ministries. They came from different walks of life and with vastly different social standing-married, divorced, professionally occupied, self-employed, childless, widowed and single. They all shared similar stories of heart-breaking pain and well-hidden deep-rooted shame. They were all looking for healing and acceptance, seeking for a way to shut the door on the fear and sorrow that tainted their joy and expectation for a new lease of life. Some of their pain was raw and for others it was a deep seated constant ache arising out of chronic wounds. Their stories were brutal and sad but what was heart-breaking was that the church did not dwell on their issues it felt as though the silence of the church pointed directly to the denial of the pain they endured.

It wounded me deeply to see so many women struggling with their pain carefully masked behind well-rehearsed cliché statements of faith because they were not secure enough to express their true feelings not only to a judgemental world but also to a judgemental religious community. The church knew of their struggles and the shame they battled but church leaders would not openly discuss it because they feared that corporate faith would be diminished in the face of the scourge of violence against women. Marital separation and divorce were widely frowned upon in religious circles and so many women suffered in silence in desperate situations. So the silence of the church only grew louder while the pain of those living in fear and shame only grew deeper. I was frustrated at the complicit silence of the church. I had watched my mother drown in the silence of her pain until the danger of losing her life had motivated her to find the courage and strength to remove herself and her children from the clutches of death. The church had known the danger she was in or at the very least other church members had known but they had turned a blind eye to her trauma. How many women would be unlucky enough to fail to escape the danger? How many children would be scarred by the violence taking place behind closed doors before they were placed in safety? I urged ministry leaders to speak about it and to lend a voice to the voiceless who felt they had no escape from the terror and the pain. Religious leaders had to extend their influence to issues affecting the broken men and women in their communities who were raising sons and daughters who would only perpetuate the cycle of violence in their adulthood. Violence begets more violence. The narrative had to change before it was too late.

> 'I URGED MINISTRY LEADERS TO SPEAK ABOUT IT AND TO LEND A VOICE TO THE VOICELESS WHO FELT THEY HAD NO ESCAPE FROM THE TERROR AND THE PAIN.'

I began to speak at women's meetings, sharing my experience and adding my voice to the growing discontent of how women's issues were quietly ignored and only spoken of in hushed tones outside the confines of the church buildings. The stain of shame that haunted the broken survivors of violence had to be exposed as the complete lie that it was.

I risked being misunderstood and labelled a feminist yet again but I had to push against the resistance to raise the profile of the plight of victimised women. I knew how traumatic it was to feel invisible while I bled to death inwardly because until recently I was a broken woman too. My mother had known the same pain too and my children had seen it. Three generations in my family had not been spared and it had to stop. I knew only too well the hollow pain of living without hope in a cruel world. My voice only became louder.

It had been three years since I had moved to South Africa. Thami was 8 years old and Nkosi was 5, ready to start school. I had only seen them three times in the past 3 years I had been away, always at Christmas. I had missed so many firsts of their childhood. I could no longer miss any more moments in the rest of their growth and development as they grew older. I decided to move back home and continue with my ministry work while I raised my children. My work would not stop. I would carry on the fight only this time I would bring it closer to home. There were broken women and children in Zimbabwe too. I would lend my voice to their fight.

I soon realised that life in Zimbabwe was difficult; more difficult than I had realised on my short visits over the past 3 years during the Christmas season when the general mood was lively and festive. Unemployment was higher as was the cost of living. The prices of basic goods were sky rocketing and out of reach for the masses who earned well below the basic wage. As the economy imploded so did the social structures of the communities that the people lived in. The purchase power of middle class incomes plummeted as poverty engulfed families. Children were turned away from schools as parents failed to pay the escalating costs of a basic education. Those who managed to pay the term fees could hardly meet the costs of stationery, uniforms and school development levies. To compound this, the ravaging effects of the HIV/AIDS pandemic tore through communities leaving young orphans in the care of their ageing grandparents for those who were fortunate to have living grandparents. However, the frailty of their grandparents often exceeded their ability to adequately care for their young wards leaving them to fend for themselves. Family structures crumbled as relatives turned these vulnerable children away and economic responsibility for the orphaned households fell on the shoulders of young children-some as young as twelve or thirteen.

I noticed more children on the streets than I had ever seen growing up. Street children, was the term used to describe this social anomaly. These defenceless children would fall prey to illicit drug use, alcohol abuse, sexual violence and prostitution. One such community which was affected by the decay of the family unit resulting in the emergence of child led households was Epworth, an informal settlement on the eastern outskirts of Harare which I visited regularly in ministry work. Created by the migration of desperate young rural dwellers drawn to Harare in search of employment the sprawling settlement developed haphazardly. Roads, buildings and schools sprouted as improvised structures. The settlement struggled with overcrowding, lack of basic services and food security. Children were vulnerable, especially underage girls who often dropped out of school as they fell pregnant. Underage marriages were rampant in this neglected community.

Overwhelmed by the loss of innocence and exploited vulnerability I saw I began to think of ways I could help the children in Epworth. I shared this with Judith one Saturday afternoon ahead of her return to South Africa. She had travelled to Zimbabwe to visit her parents who still lived in the country. The day before she was due to fly back to South Africa she paid me a visit. She asked about my plans and if I was going to continue to stay in Zimbabwe. She had noticed the dereliction and decay creeping into the communities. As I spoke about the plight of the forgotten children in Epworth wallowing in abject poverty oblivious to the possibilities which lay just outside their small community my voice trembled with emotion. Judy's compassionate gaze fell on my distraught face as I continued. When I stopped to wipe the tears which involuntarily trickled down my face she leaned over and held my hand.

"You want to do something about this issue of the children. Talk to me Shumi. What are you thinking?"

I poured out my heart, the helplessness I felt as poverty drowned the children in Epworth. The ministry work I did was not helping as many children as I wanted. My efforts were like the ripples of a pebble in an ocean. The problem was far bigger than a one-woman band could carry. I needed more hands and more voices. She listened as I described what I would do if I had the resources to do more. I would build a school which would be a safe haven for all children and no child would be denied an education. That would be the primary mandate of the school; to never turn a child away. I would also provide a meal at school for every child and the school would be a place of hope and healing as it would be a place for learning. Every child would have a chance at going after their dreams.

> YOU'RE A TEACHER AND A MINISTER BUT YOU'RE ALSO A HUMANITARIAN AND YOU'RE A FIGHTER.

"Build the school Shumi" Judith said quietly when I had finished speaking. "You can't stand pain and injustice. Pain feeds your drive for change. You're a teacher and a minister but you're also a humanitarian and you're a fighter. In fact, you're whatever the season you're in demands! You won't take no so get up and get this done!"

I wiped my face as I looked at her. The intensity in her gaze revived my flagging spirits.

"I wouldn't know where to begin Judy."

"Collaboration. You can't do this alone. I can help you register an OVC organisation which simply means an Orphans and Vulnerable Children community based organisation. You'll need to come up with a clear vision and a statement of intent outlining what you want to achieve and a set of tangible goals to work towards in accomplishing your mission." She paused and smiled at the growing excitement that I was beginning to show.

"Well that's the fun part. The hard part is getting supporters. You will need dream builders and vision partners; people who are completely invested in your vision. These will be the people who are committed to go for the long haul on these kids in order to help give them a future. They have to see what you see when you look at the children and be willing to commit time and money."

The rest of the afternoon was spent in detailing a plan of action to register a community based organisation. She called two contacts she knew who worked in the Social Work Department in Harare and they outlined the necessary steps I would have to take in order to establish a non-profit for disadvantaged children. I would also need a board of directors and I had just the right people in mind whom I knew would be capable of helping to build the school.

"What will you call the organisation?" Judith asked.

It was all about the children; the forgotten children of my beloved country...

"Mwana" I answered softly. *Mwana* means child in the local Shona dialect. "That's a great name" she smiled.

It was several months before all the paperwork was completed. In the months preceding the registration of Mwana I was able to canvas for support among prominent leaders and organisations in the social services sector. I was elated when several of the influential forerunners I approached agreed to be part of the board of Mwana. I had specialists in various fields ranging from education, media and communication as well as in the banking and finance sectors. I could hardly believe that I had such expertise at my disposal in the building of this dream which I held dear. Mwana was about extending hope to a generation of children who were without hope and without a future. I would need all the help I could get to restore the balance in their broken lives.

It was a long and difficult road to the fulfilment of the vision. The school was finally built one year later, a simple wooden structure on a piece of land allocated by the Epworth council offices. I started off with ten children and soon word spread that there was a free meal at Mwana and more children trekked in as the challenges mounted. I struggled to cater for them and to solve the myriad of problems my young wards had to contend with on a daily basis-no food, no shelter and no hope. I struggled to sleep at night as I lay in the dark, contemplating the darkness they lived in perpetually. I struggled and I was overwhelmed but I did not give up.

The construction of the classroom cabins had to be expanded to cater for the swelling numbers. I needed more teachers for the growing number of classes. I also needed more volunteers to cook the afternoon meal for the children. I reached out to friends and colleagues in the teaching community. They enlisted in the work of rebuilding the community, one child at a time. I approached the mothers within Epworth to volunteer at the school and soon they had a working roster for volunteer cooks. With the board members driving the fundraising initiative I was able to maintain a steady supply of food for the supplementary feeding for my wards. At the end of each day when classes were over, the last meal served and no child turned away I was grateful for yet another fruitful day. My measure of success was in each tooth-gapped smile I saw as they waved their teachers goodbye at the end of the day.

As the months sped by my own life was changed by my young wards at Mwana. My own sons were growing, Thami who was now in high school was in a boarding school in Gweru and Nkosi who was 12 was also at the same boarding school studying for his grade 7 examinations, the final year of primary education. I relocated from my home in the middle class suburb of Westgate to modest lodgings near the school in Epworth during the school term when my sons would be away in school. My friends soon became the women who sold at the makeshift market stalls just outside the school. They lived in poverty stricken conditions, survivors of harrowing tales of lack, abuse and powerlessness and yet they smiled. They still found reason to be joyful in the face of adversity. They soon became my heroes and I would sit on a plastic bucket in the dusty streets of Epworth and marvel at their tenacity as they shared their stories. They would laugh and clap their hands oblivious to the decay surrounding them. They lived each day in modest triumph over their fears and pain. There was always the threat of a new challenge and a bigger fight but they never gave up. Every single day they chose to focus on the fight of the present. To my new friends, worrying about the future was an exercise in futility as the future was not promised to all. Suffice each day its own problems and its own joys was their attitude.

I immersed myself in the lives of my wards as the months merged into years. Mwana grew in influence and impact in the local community as more children continued to stream into the school for education and hope. Drug use had escalated among the youth as economic woes rippled through the country. The youth in Epworth were not spared as they turned to the intoxicating highs of drug induced altered mental states to escape the reality of the misery of their existence. Drug peddlers profited at the expense of an entire generation of young people whose dreams were shattered, their eyes glazed over as they staggered through the streets. I noticed the slow death creep into my new home of Epworth; the chemically induced stupor which was stealing our children and the future of our nation. I had to fight back.

I harnessed local law enforcement in my fight against substance abuse. I canvassed the streets, engaging all I met, both young and old. I leveraged the contacts I had made in my outreach campaigns and informal community meetings with local community members. I lived with them and I was now one of them, so they trusted me. The inroads I had made in establishing relationships within the community were finally paying off. Soon I had enough information to get the shadowy syndicates operating within the settlement arrested for drug trafficking. There was a war on our hands. Instrumental in whistleblowing and exposing the trail of criminal drug trafficking I soon became a target for frustrated drug peddlers. I received death threats and some of my teaching staff were harassed. I took the death threats seriously and went into hiding as investigations were underway only emerging after the culprits had been arrested. Each time an arrest was made I was encouraged. One peddler at a time the streets would be made safe for our children. I was committed to the fight but a bigger fight loomed on the horizon. A fight I was not prepared for.

# CHAPTER 19

The headaches were getting worse. I had always struggled with migraines which had been a recurring affliction for years since the arrival of my second child. I knew the symptoms well and had a ready supply of Migral on hand. The onset of neck pain and stiffness followed by nausea would signal the advent of a migraine attack. Hours later an excruciating throbbing in the front part of my head would leave me irritable, sluggish and fatigued. Medication accompanied with rest in bed in a darkened room relieved the painful effects of the migraine attack. I experienced these attacks at least monthly. Lately however the attacks were becoming more frequent and the pain unbearable. The blinding pain and debilitating exhaustion needed medical attention.

I was placed on a more potent pain prescription when I initially went to consult my doctor. Weeks later I was back in the doctor's office complaining of severe pain and incidents of temporary blindness. The first incident had occurred when I was in class as I was teaching. As I turned to the chalkboard behind me a thick darkness enveloped me. I could hear the quiet chatter of the students and even the distant laughter of the vendors who sat at the gate selling their wares to passers-by. With rising panic, I rubbed my eyes and opened them, blinking desperately. The darkness closed in. I groped at the darkness as I stumbled towards the door calling for help. Upon hearing my cries one of the mothers who were cooking outside rushed to my side and she led me across the grounds and seated me on a reed mat under a shady tree. I had to regain control of the terror welling up inside of me. I still could not see anything but the dense blackness clawing at me. I closed my eyes and breathed deeply.

I could feel the sun on my skin where gaps in the branches of the tree I was sitting under gave way to the rays shining through. I willed myself to listen to the sounds around me; the chirping of the birds, the gentle rustling of the leaves above me as the branches swayed gently in the summer breeze, the squeals of worn brakes as a car sped past the school on the dusty terrain that was a makeshift road. I took another deep breath and the aroma of the dusty earth intermingled with woody pines and Musasa trees filled my nostrils. I opened my eyes and caught my breath as the glare of the sun filled my line of vision. I smiled as the familiar horizon of the school came into focus. Relieved I stood up and headed back to the classroom where my students waited but my head was still pounding.

Dr Moyo had kind but probing eyes. His forehead was creased in consternation as he surveyed the notes in his hands.

"Temporary blindness isn't uncommon in severe migraine attacks" he said softly. "But I think we need to do more tests."

He pulled a pad off a stack of papers piled high on his desk and began writing as he continued speaking.

"It's best we err on the side of caution so I'll be referring you for a CT Scan and more blood work."

"Should I be worried doctor?" I asked directly. "My life is busy now and I need to focus on real problems. Will I be able to take care of my responsibilities with minimum disruption?"

"Well the sooner we get to the cause of your headaches and deal with the problem the sooner you can get on with your real problems" he chuckled as he handed me the test request.

The tests were scheduled for later that afternoon and as the appointment time drew closer my head began to ache. The radiologist was a cheerful elderly professor who shared quirky academic jokes as he prepped me for the examination. He rightly surmised my reticence for discomfort and gently asked how bad the pain was. It was his tone of kindness coupled with the helplessness I felt as the pulsating pain in my head throbbed relentlessly that touched a nerve and tears filled my eyes. Mortified I hurriedly wiped my face and tried to smile. He smiled back.

"Let's get you feeling better by getting this test done shall we." He said as he began the testing process.

I woke up feeling stronger the following day. The heaviness I was accustomed to was visibly absent when I shook my head from side to side. The rest of the day held so much promise for hopeful news. I was relaxed and pain free, a state. I was no longer used to. It was going to be a good day. I had an appointment with Dr Moyo later that morning. My friend and Mwana school administrator Leo Hama had cleared his schedule for the day in order to drive me into town. I had met Leo upon my return to Zimbabwe and he had proved to be an invaluable ally in establishing Mwana. He picked me up from the school at 9am and he stopped at one of my favourite bakery outlets to order a cup of herbal tea and a slice of lemon cake ahead of my 1030AM appointment.

"To celebrate you" he said laughing at my surprised face. "I'm expecting a good outcome with your test results today. "A celebration!" I smiled back in agreement. From where I sat the sun appeared from behind a cloud, its rays casting a luminescent glow across the face of the sky. I was happy and I had never felt more alive.

I sat in the high backed chair across the desk from Dr Moyo, my racing thoughts clamouring louder and louder in my head. My hands were clasped tightly in my lap as I tried to still the scream that was rising within me. I tried to release my balled fists but I knew the shaking would start. The tremors would cascade up my arms and soon my whole body would yield to the growing fear in me as I trembled uncontrollably. I had to stay afloat and not succumb to the weight of the terror and fear. If only the voices in my head would stop shouting. I shut my eyes in despair.

"What are you saying Dr Moyo?" my voice barely above a whisper in the quiet office.

"The CT Scan results show a localised abnormal growth in your brain, a mass." He shuffled the papers on his desk as he paused. "We will have to run more tests in order to define the tumour and possibly grade it if it turns out to be malignant. This will help determine the treatment options available for you to commence."

"I have cancer!" my voice broke as a flood of emotions erupted. My head throbbed in pain as the tears flowed. My worst fears were confirmed. *Cancer*. The dreaded six letter  diagnosis which haunted humanity and evaded scientific advancements and quantum leaps in technology to wreak pain and hopelessness while leaving a trail of death in its wake. I woke up in the middle of the night choking in fear at the prospect of dying when I still desperately wanted to live. I still had much to do. I had a fight against an uncaring world for the children I had grown to love and care for at Mwana. I needed them, probably more than they needed me, because they gave me reason to hope that God would give me a second chance to live for their sake. Would they have another advocate if I died? I was not ready to die.

As the days merged into weeks I became angry. I felt let down and victimised. My life had been a series of pain, struggle and tragedy replayed over and over again in different scenarios. I was tired and angry and I had neither the strength nor the will to fight left. This battle was too big and the odds stacked high against me. Slowly I began to fantasise about dying as the headaches worsened. The pain would seize my head in a vice like grip for hours on end. Hours slipped into days and time was lost in a sea of unrelenting pain. Those were the bad days and they were frequent. On the *'good'* days I would wake up with a slight throbbing in my head and I would feel almost like my old self again. The *'good'* days were becoming more infrequent as the bad days filled up the passing weeks and months. I had to learn to co-exist with the death that was now a part of my life.

> 'IN THE SILENCE OF MY DARKENED BEDROOM I RECONNECTED TO THE CREATOR OF MY LIFE. IN THE SILENCE OF MY PAIN I FOUND MY VOICE AGAIN AND I SPOKE TO GOD THROUGH THE TEARS AS I RELEASED MY FEARS.'

My vision for Mwana still had much to be accomplished. I was running out of time. I had to do as much as possible in the little time I had left. I devised a plan to take work efficiently, taking on more complex tasks on the rare *'good'* days and rudimentary activities on the bad days. With a steady supply of effective and potent pain medication I could still take care of the administrative demands of the school while I worked quietly in the wooden structure we called the school office at the end of the school outbuildings. I was saddened that I could no longer teach, the effort of speaking loudly proving too much for my aching head. I needed silence to get through the day.

Silence became an ally and darkness my comfort. I would keep the curtains drawn to keep the bright sunlight out, which triggered my headaches. It was in the darkness and silence that I regained my faith. In the silence of my darkened bedroom I reconnected to the Creator of my life. In the silence of my pain I found my voice again and I spoke to God through the tears as I released my fears. As the emotions tumbled out in tear filled prayer my rage gave way to peace. The peace I felt as I poured myself out in broken words and anguished sobs soon began to quieten my racing thoughts and fears. I directed my focus on God and not on the death that challenged my life. Focus on the promise Shumi and not on the problem, I constantly reminded myself. I wanted to dwell on God's incomparable love and compassion if these were to be the last days of my life. Whatever the outcome I was at peace as I reflected on how he had always been merciful in his dealings with me.

I had survived a broken and violent home because of God's protection. His hand of mercy on my life was evident in the strength my mother had found in fighting to preserve her life and the lives of her daughters. I had not fully grasped the truth of God's mercy in a broken world because my perspective had always been wrapped up in what I thought I lacked, yearning for what was out of reach. I understood it now. I had children in my care, with living parents, who were fending for themselves as though they were orphaned. I encountered parents in my line of work who were trapped in a sordid prison of addiction, violence and promiscuity. I had recoiled in sadness and horror at the tales of horrendous abuse of children at the hands of their parents or guardians and yet God's mercy for the lost and forgotten children was still perceptible in their enduring and unflagging humanity. I saw it in their quick smiles and hopeful gazes as they sat on the dusty floors ready to learn. I felt it in their laughter and raucous chatter as they streamed onto the playgrounds at the end of the day. Though toughened by life's hardships they remained irrepressible. God's grace was evident in the miracles that surrounded me.

Buoyed by the resilience of the children who found a way to make it to school each morning in spite of the odds heavily stacked against them my hope was rekindled. My hope was not as a result of abating symptoms or renewed strength. If anything it only became more difficult to get up each morning and the struggle to eat became more challenging as I lost the battle to severe bouts of nausea. I spent countless evenings vomiting in the bathroom, weak and unable to withstand the vomiting I blacked out in my bed only to awaken the next morning in agony as my head throbbed incessantly. Combing my hair was unbearably excruciating and I had to shave my hair to avoid manipulating it and aggravating the debilitating headaches. I felt exposed and inadequate as I looked at my bald head reflected in the mirror. Would I ever feel beautiful again? Would I ever be desired by a man again?

In spite of the gruelling pain and persistent physical agony my body experienced, I became determined to wake up with a purposeful intent to do my best in each day I was privileged to see. Each day, my mind would resolve why I had to wake up and some days the reason was noble; for my sons, for Mwana, for a better future for all children. Other days it was because I could not stand to look at the same four walls in my room after yet another sleepless night. Sleep was elusive, a rare gift bestowed upon me on even more dwindling occasions. Even then those sleepless nights were never wasted. I spent many long nights poring over articles about the cancer I had. I studied articles and research studies on the Internet detailing treatment options, the likely prognostic outcomes and testimonies of cancer survivors. I had been placed on a cocktail of chemotherapy treatments which left me retching and miserable. I was constantly tired and soon began delegating more of my responsibilities to Leo. Although I was battered and exhausted I was still in the fight.

I was fortunate to have Leo during those times. He was a dear friend and brother. He shouldered more of the responsibilities and yet never lost a moment to call me or visit to find out how I was coping with the side effects of the treatment I was taking. I knew of the long hours he was spending working at the school to keep it running as he bore the brunt of my deteriorating condition with grace and compassion. I realised the true value of relationship as the battle against death raged on. Faced with the spectre of my own mortality I began to focus on making amends with those I loved but who had over the years grown distant because of distance and time. I had to find a way to make peace with those I could not bear to love anymore because it hurt too much to hold on to the pain.

As I lay in the silence of my darkened room I began to reflect on the moments of my greatest pain. My mind wandered back again to thoughts of my father-the first man who had been the source of my childhood wounds. I relived the memories of the years I had been a girl desperately yearning for the love and comfort of a stranger I called father. My mind floated through the years and faltered as the darkness of the rape surfaced. I could not bring myself to forgive Makoni for the rape. The strength to form the thoughts or words of forgiveness was completely beyond me but instead I extended the grace of self-acceptance to myself, relinquishing any blame of any wrong doing on my part. An act of self-love, I affirmed myself in spite of the loss and rejection I had endured in my life. I could not alter the events leading to the conception of my first child but I would always choose Thami in spite of the pain. I would choose him even before I chose myself. I loved my son and his paternity could never change that. Whether he was Vusi's son or not Thami was my miracle and grace. Choosing Thami meant I was choosing love and love always wins.

In choosing Thami I also chose liberty. Although I could not forgive Makoni I found the courage to release his memory. Whatever demons had stolen his humanity from him were his to face. Vengeance was not my way. I found that the release came with peace when I finally surrendered the vengeful thoughts which had swirled in my mind for years. It was not the kind of peace which filled me with comfort and strength. Instead I found a form of peace which freed me from pursuing Makoni in the dark recesses of my mind in a bloody act of vengeance which replayed itself over and over again and allowed me to breathe fully again. The shadows where he had lurked in my dreams faded as hope expanded obliterating the seeds of hate he had sowed. His power was finally diminished. I was no longer a captive to fear.

I released Vusi too and all he had done to me. He was the father of my sons and he had embraced Thami as his own and that would never change. He still cared for both Thami and Nkosi without impartiality. I could not erase all that Vusi had been to me during my first pregnancy, a source of comfort, hope and strength. I had given Vusi all of my love, the grown kind of love on which we could have built a real future and we had tried to make it last. At least I had and the love Vusi had shown me for the first three years of our marriage was the whole conversation I had longed to have about true love while growing up; a conversation about intimacy, trust, vulnerability and generosity. A conversation so riveting it captured me as the layers peeled away to reveal more beautiful depths hidden beneath the surface but sadly it was a conversation which had ended all too soon. There had been too many secrets in our love, too much darkness to hide from the light and the darkness had surfaced in Vusi in ways that were eerily similar to what had surfaced in my father. Vusi's love which had been my restoration had fallen apart to reveal a deep brokenness that could not be healed by any effort on my part. Desperation has a way of blinding us to the faults of those we love deeply. Marrying Vusi had left me desperately yearning for wholeness which I found when I finally walked from our toxic marriage. As the nights closed in on me in silence, I yielded to my vulnerability and forgave him. I forgave him for the long years of abuse, lost hope, fear and shame. I forgave him for the darkness which had plagued him and wounded us, driving us apart. The silence folded around me as I lay in bed and I was at peace at last.

# CHAPTER 20

 settled back in my seat as the bus pulled out of the station heading south of the city. The incandescent city lights danced in the distance as the bus cruised onto the motorway. I glanced at the luminous dial on my watch in semi-darkness of the bus interior. It was 8:15PM. Most of the passengers were already beginning to doze off. I couldn't sleep however despite the sedatives and pain medication I had taken just before departure. My body craved rest but my mind was alert as the thoughts raced through my mind. I was on my way to Johannesburg, South Africa to consult a specialist doctor in the field of Oncology. It would have been a better alternative to take a flight to South Africa as the trip by road would take close to 12 hours but I could not afford a flight. My financial situation was strained, more-so with all the treatment payments I was making from my monthly stipend from the school. A return fare by bus was all I could afford for which I was grateful. Dr Moyo had advised against a long bus trip but he eventually relented when I explained that most of the trip would take place overnight and that I would be asleep for the most part of the journey. He had prescribed sedatives and analgesics to tide me over during the trip. Soon I began to feel drowsy as the medication took effect. I slipped into a dreamless slumber as the bus rolled into the night.

It was just after 1AM when I woke up with a start. A wave of nausea washed over me as struggled to sit upright. The throbbing in my head intensified. I doubled over groaning inaudibly. Another wave of nausea engulfed me. The sedatives were wearing off and my body was wracked with pain. The passengers seated next to me were casting concerned glances in my direction.

"Are you alright?" the elderly lady sitting across the aisle asked, her brow furrowed with worry.

"I'm fine" I replied with a weak grin, dismally failing in my attempt to disguise my obvious discomfort. Grunting I leaned over in my seat, clutching the seat armrests as the throbbing in my head extended to the front of my face. Darkness swirled as I slumped in my seat.

I woke up to the sound of mechanical beeping and purring of hospital equipment on a side table next to me. I was in a brightly lit hospital room with sea green blinds covering the windows at the end of the room. I could not remember how I had ended up here. The last memory I had was of the blackness enveloping me on the bus. The bus! Where was my luggage! I groped for support as I attempted to pull myself up. I caught my breath as pain exploded in my head. The beeping increased ominously.

The door swung open as a nurse strode in. She smiled reassuringly as she picked up my arm to check my pulse.

"Welcome back to the world!" Her lively voice filled the room.

"Where am I?" my own voice a hoarse whisper.

"You're in hospital Ma'am."

I looked at her quizzically wondering how I had arrived at the hospital.

"You were brought in unconscious but we found your medical history in your bag. That was a stroke of good luck that you carried it! Don't worry Ma'am more will be explained once the doctor gets here. Get some rest" she reassured me. She administered what must have been a sedative because soon I felt a languor sweep over my body as I slipped into an uneasy slumber.

I was hospitalised for a week at the end of which I was transferred to the Oncology Clinic as an outpatient. Complete with my medical history from Dr Moyo I was commenced on radiotherapy sessions while continuing with my chemotherapy treatment which had been adjusted to include a new regimen of drugs. Dr Mary Hill, my new doctor explained that the treatment would be more aggressive in countering the growth of the tumour in my head. The battery of che-mo-radiotherapy treatments took their toll on my health, physically and emotionally. My hair fell out in chunks and I lost a great deal of weight. Food lost all flavour and I spent many hours doubled over the toilet seat, retching in agony.

I was in Johannesburg for 3 months under the care of Dr Mary Hill. It was a long period of feeling wretched and I was constantly on the verge of despair. Stretching on for what seemed like interminable days I wept disconsolately as my pulverised body succumbed to the side effects of the chemotherapy. My body was pumped full of powerful chemotherapy drugs at each appointment. Exhausted, bloated and sometimes hopeless I struggled to attend my appointments. My whole body ached but my will to live was still stronger than my willingness to give up. Death would have been kind at this very low point in my life and I courted the idea of giving up but in spite of the trauma and discomfort I was going through I held on desperately to life. I still had much to do. I was not ready yet.

As I struggled with the physical pain and the psychological trauma of therapy, I felt alone and isolated in the world. I was alone in a foreign country and my family could not be with me. They could not afford the cost of living in South Africa for an indefinite period of time and so I had to weather the bruising fight and make a stand against the death sentence handed me. On the brink of despair, it soon became apparent to me that I was not alone as I had a new family in this strange land; strangers in uniforms to help me. They were the nurses, doctors, pharmacists and orderlies designated to help me fight the greatest battle of my life. It was easier slipping, falling and giving up in their company. There were no expectations, no disappointment but only support and hope fuelled inspiration to keep fighting. When I crumbled in frustration on the verge of giving up, there were no recrim- inations, only compassion. I was grateful for their care and dedication as the disease ravaged my body. I often thought of my sons. Whenever I cried out to God to take me I would think of Thami and Nkosi and my anguished sobs would cease. It was in these dark moments that I was most thankful for the distance between us. They were spared from watching my body waste away and the light in my eyes vanish.

I had taught my sons love, generosity and service. Through my own life and the many battles I had fought, I had taught them about the triumph of faith over fear and hope over grief. I could not give up now because my surrender would deliver a crushing blow to their fragile faith. They were still young and although they were hardly boys, they were almost men-Thami was 18 and Nkosi 15-they still needed just a little more time. The assurance of my love and the stead- fastness of my presence would be a comfort for them for a while, until they I was ready to let them go. I carried the anguish of every mother. I could not leave them in the world to face life on their own, not just yet. I spoke to them most evenings when I was not feeling too unwell to talk. Thami always ended our conversations with affirmation of my healing. The faith I had the God who had created me would have to hold out for both their sakes, and if I was completely honest, for my sake too. I had unfulfilled plans for my own life too. I wanted to grow Mwana into a self-sufficient organisation and thereby secure a sustainable future for my wards. I wanted to watch my sons grow and fall in love and one day hold my grandchildren in my arms. I still hoped to one day find a love of my own. These were my yearnings and I needed more time.

I was not always brave or hopeful but I tried to remember to say yes to life. In spite of my determination and resolve to stay hopeful, my body continued to react adversely to the new drug regimen. I developed painful reactions to radiotherapy treatments and hardly felt the numbing effect of pain medication which only left me more nauseous than relieved of the pain coursing through my body. I lay writhing on the floor in my room after therapy and my skin became a patch-work of burns and scars. I had bald patches on my scalp which once was covered with tightly coiled natural curls. My beauty was gone, youthfulness and the full bloom of vitality retreating in the face of the aggressive treatment. Yet I still held onto life and love and the hope they represented. I held onto the love of my sons who still needed me. I held onto my dreams because with them I could keep on believing that a miracle was possible. I held on to the love of my mother who prayed for me pleading that my life would be spared and that I would find the miracle in more health, more joy and more peace. I clung to the love of friends like Judith and Leo who refused to believe in anything else but life in all its abundance for me. Love held me as the battle raged on.

---

 formatting separator: &infin;

This felt familiar, the bright city lights fading into the distance as the bus roared down the highway into the inky darkness of the night. I touched my head. It was wrapped in a brightly coloured turban just like Matron MaHungwe used to wear when I was in boarding school. I had different coloured turbans which I was accustomed to wearing now since the loss of my hair. I smiled. I hoped my sons would love the colourful head-wraps. There was no sharp pain in my head and even the familiar nausea which would rise from the pit of my stomach was gone. All I could feel was the gentle rising in my chest as I breathed quietly in the darkened bus. I closed my eyes as I recalled my last consultation with the doctor the previous week.

---

&

---

I was sitting on a chair in Dr Mary Hill's demurely decorated office. She wore a strange expression on her usually smiling face and my heart raced in fear. My latest diagnostic scan results were back. Was the cancer failing to respond to the treatment I wondered gloomily. I was too afraid to voice my fears.

"Your results are here Shumi" her soft voice cut into my tumultuous thoughts. "It looks like preliminary results indicate remission."

My thoughts tumbled wildly in my head. REMISSION! Did she just say REMISSION? Startled I bolted out of my chair.

"Did you say remission Dr Mary?" I stuttered, uncertain as hope flailed in intermittent waves of anxiety and elation.

She smiled a full, wide-eyed and gentle smile. "Yes!" she breathed excitedly. "Remission!"

"I don't understand!" I exclaimed. "I thought I'd need more sessions of chemo-radiotherapy!"

"That makes two of us who don't understand how this tumour responded so well to the new drug regimen when all indications pointed to a mediocre outcome and extended therapy. But the results are more than excellent so far! Not to raise your hopes too high but this is amazing! Of course you will need regular reviews till we're absolutely certain you're in the clear but as for today I can say you are cancer free Shumi!"

My knees buckled underneath me and I slumped to the floor as the tears gushed down my face. Dr Mary rushed to my side.

"It's alright" I whispered through my tears. "I just need a moment. This is God! He saved me when I was almost giving up. He saved me for my boys and my children at Mwana. He saved me for a reason and He did it when I thought it was all over for me." She nodded her head understandingly as she slipped to her knees next to me and there we both knelt on the floor-a doctor and her patient, two women giving thanks for a miracle.

I was in remission! A miracle I was still grasping but even then I knew that the miracle had started long before the final results. The payment for my treatment regimens were a miracle too. Unable to afford my consultations at the hospital for the protracted length of my stay in South Africa, funds had been sourced from well-wishers and friends. I called them destiny helpers because they had helped to keep the purpose I was created for alive. Financial deposits were made into an account which had been set up with a local bank in South Africa and the amounts received weekly always adequately covered my medical bills at the time of receipt. I never asked for the money and I never sent an invoice. The miracles were evident in every notification I received when the money was posted into my account. My hospital bills had always been paid on time.

---

&

I opened my eyes and glanced at my watch. It was 10:05PM. I was heading back home and the thought filled me with peace. I smiled as I reflected on the journey that had led me here. I thought of my mother, a scarred woman who loved imperfectly but who loved fiercely in her quiet and restrained way. Ours had been a tumultuous relationship and through the years we had wounded each other but we were making room for healing. I knew where the root of my deepest hurt lay. It was in how I had always felt that I did not measure up to her expectations and how I felt too different from the woman who had given me life. Yet now that I was older I realised how similar we both were. Her tenacity and determination mirrored in my single mindedness as I pursued my purpose. I was a reflection of the virtues that had led her on her own journey of purpose. I loved her but our love was a dance that had kept us at arm's length as we navigated our pain. I was ready to hold her closer now that I knew what she saw when she looked at me; her own reflection in my eyes. I was my mother's daughter. I settled back in the seat and sighed as sleep stole over me. I was going home.

# EPILOGUE

**A**s we ushered in the New Year, on 1 January 2021 I received the call. My friend and pillar, dear Uncle Francis was gone. He was the man I had called father when my own stopped being a father to me. Present at my marriage negotiations, he had welcomed Vusi into the family with laughter and tight hugs all round, unheard of in our formal culture and way of life. He had stood up for me when my own life had crumbled around me after my marriage to Vusi ended. A staunch supporter of my non-profit work, he had always been encouraging about my work at Mwana when the rest of my family could not understand why I was giving up my whole life for broken and unwanted children. He understood why I was building a life in a forgotten part of the country. He had also celebrated when I returned home three years ago, cancer free and healthy. Laughingly he had said that he would charge a special cow for my dowry at my marriage negotiations when I found a man lucky enough to marry me. "You're unbeatable Shumi; *mukuwasha* (the groom) must pay for such enduring resilience!" Uncle Francis had died from Covid-19, a deadly disease which had emerged late in 2019 and ravaged the world.

Two years before the devastation wrought by Covid-19, the world had celebrated me for a year. It was uncomfortable and unnatural at first to be at the centre of global attention because I had not started this work for the awards and accolades but I was grateful for the visibility our purpose was contributing to the neglected in the community. Recognized internationally as a mother to over a thousand boys and girls, at Mwana Worldwide, the citations and accolades began to pour in. I had overcome great personal adversity to become a champion for the voiceless in our work with vulnerable children. Mwana Worldwide had spread its reach beyond Harare to other towns and cities in the country. As the world took interest in the work we were doing in these communities, I found myself hosted by various international institutions at receptions in London, Lagos and Nairobi. I shared platforms with prominent scholars and African Premiers as I led discussions on the impact of the work Mwana Worldwide was doing. I was humbled to be named Humanitarian of the year at a ceremony in Dar-es-Salam and the following year, an online publication listed me as one of the top 10 emerging influential women in Africa. After the meetings and speeches, the real work still lay in ensuring that the children we served were getting the education and security necessary for them to have a future to look forward to. The emergence of Covid-19 posed a risk to that future.

Uncertainty and fear gripped the world as the devastating effects of the second wave of the Corona virus epidemic rippled throughout the world in late 2020, leaving death and untold misery in its trail. The world was plunged into another lockdown as travel was restricted and borders closed in an attempt to curb the spread of the disease. On the 4th of January 2021 Zimbabwe's streets were deserted as the country braced itself for another bruising battle with the relentless virus. I had to isolate from my family as I had begun to feel unwell after Uncle Francis' funeral. Treatment for Covid-19 was experimental as investigations on treatment options were still underway in different parts of the world. I struggled with abdominal pain and fatigue, whether from the illness or from the treatment I do not know, but I persisted in completing the full course of treatment. It was the mental anguish of isolation itself which hurt me more than the mild illness I was struggling with. I was one of the lucky ones. I had never seen so much death and I cried angry tears as messages of friends and family burying their loved ones poured in.

17 January 2021 I was dealt another blow which left me reeling in unbearable pain. Robert, my best friend, partner and soul mate gave up his fight against Covid-19 after a ten-day battle. Heart-broken I cried for death to take me too. There was no purpose in continuing on without the man who had become the centre of my world. I had met Robert three months after my return from South Africa through a mutual friend. He was a surgeon with a busy practice in Harare. Divorced with two beautiful children from his previous marriage, he was a devout Christian who also loved adventure and we spent his few free afternoons with his children, exploring the local safari adventures on the outskirts of the city. We went canoeing on the lake located just outside Harare, horseback riding at the Game Park north of the city and reluctantly visited the Snake Park where he shared extensive knowledge on reptiles. Initially I had resisted his attentions believing that a man of his social standing and with his good looks and charm would have no shortage of attractive female company. I was hardly a catch, a survivor of cancer and an unemployed single parent. Robert was both persistent and patient, gently disarming me of any residual fears I had about yielding to the growing feelings I had for him.

He was fully committed to me and he showed me love in ways I had never thought possible. He would randomly call in the middle of the day to ask if I had eaten because he knew that I was accustomed to skipping meals as I pursued deadlines and attended meetings during busy days. He knew the intricate details of my schedule and often he would show up just to hug me and remind me that he loved me. He often brought a package of sweet treats and confectionery which he knew I loved most. I looked forward to each new sunrise and I walked with a spring in my step. I was healthy, happy and most importantly I was in love. The last time I had been this happy was when I had brought my children into the world. Finally, I had been given a second chance at finding fulfilment and my joy was complete.

When Robert started talking about meeting my family I was nervous and excited. He was a modern man and yet he was charmingly old fashioned in many ways. He would hold my hand in public and he had no qualms in demonstrating his affection towards me in warm hugs and slow kisses and yet he insisted that we consummate our relationship on our wedding night. Recently he had expressed his intention to commit to me as a husband. "It's not a proposal yet" he smilingly said as he took my hands in his somehow managing to look both playful and serious at the same time. "But consider it a pre-notification of a proper proposal after I meet your family Ms Kawa." The meeting with Aunt Jo had been set for the 21st of January. He died four days before the day he would have met my family.

I could not attend the funeral because I was still in quarantine. My shattered heart could not make sense of the reality of his death and I could not bear the thought that I would never see him again. My heart lurched in anguish at the thought that I would never feel his hand on the small of my waist as we walked together, that I would never hear his voice call me Ms Kawa as he was fond of doing. I would never see his face crease into a wide smile when I would call him Cupcake. I sat in the semi darkness of my bedroom weeping brokenly as I imagined the darkness closing in on him in death while he suffered alone. He had sent a text message on his phone the night before he took his final breath. It was a simple message.

*11:55pm*
*I love you today and forever my sweet Shue.*

*11:58pm*
*I love you eternally my Cupcake. I had responded.*

He later died in the early hours of the morning at 03:30am

I am standing today. It has been a little over two weeks since my darling Robert passed. I still wake up half expecting him to call and tell me he missed me during the night and how he cannot wait to be my husband. I miss him calling me during the long days at the school to remind me to eat when my schedule is busy. I miss him when I am home in the evenings scrolling through the television channels for something to watch and I catch the tail end of a wildlife programme 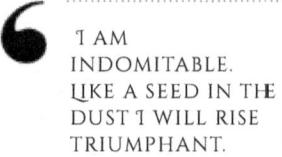 about reptiles. I miss him unexpectedly in the middle of the day when I am surrounded by people and I scan the room for his familiar profile. His death broke me but I am rebuilding again. I walk towards the window and look at the clearing skies. The storm has passed and the earth has been washed in clear waters soaking deep into the soil. I am unbeatable. I am indomitable. Like a seed in the dust I will rise triumphant. I will rise

"THE DESIRE TO REACH THE
STARS IS AMBITIOUS.
THE DESIRE TO REACH HEARTS
IS WISE AND MOST POSSIBLE."

(MAYA ANGELOU)

"A Seed in the Dust" is Ruramai Nyadzayo-Mugwisi's first book. It was written over 10 months during a period when the world faced fear and uncertainty in the wake of the global Covid-19 pandemic. Ruramai also faced her own personal struggles during the same time, recovering from major surgery and an up close and terrifying encounter with Covid-19.

Ruramai is a girl and women's empowerment champion, a poet, spoken word artist, digital content creator, medical scientist, wife and mother to four amazing children. Ruramai is a devoted Christian and passionate about purposeful and mindful living.

# ACKNOWLEDGEMENTS

Pastor Cynthia Chirinda—for your selfless devotion and impactful work in bringing this book to the world.

To my publishers Wholeness Incorporated Publishing-for the tireless commitment to excellence.

James—my loving husband, my heartbeat and soul mate. Doing life with you is a never-ending adventure. Thank you for sitting up with me late into the night proof reading, formatting and doing all the digital tech things to get the manuscript ready in time. I love you.

My children—Ruvarashe, Thabonga, Ruth and Tanaka-you are my inspiration to keep breathing and to never stop striving. You make the sun shine a little brighter in my world.

Mom and Dad—your love, unending wisdom and persistent prayers are my anchor.

My sister Yolanda, my 'almost twin' Tafadzwa, the 'family ency- clopaedia' Tatenda and Kuzivakwashe for your generous love, support and constancy in my life.

Rumbidzai Judith Kamba—you inspired an awakening of dreams long forgotten

My circle and sisterhood—Nozwelo Ndebele, Bernania Tapfuma, Rumbi Muzvarwandoga, Angela Takavarasha, Lucy Samuriwo, Faith Chahuruva, Ruvimbo Mazikana, Kundai Sithole, Faith Mukuku and Rebecca Kanoerera—for your grace, patience wisdom and comfort when I needed them most.

## ACKNOWLEDGEMENTS

My trusted allies—'Ma' Ethel Ngema (my earthly guardian angel), Christine Moyo and Dilean Mkwananzi,

Julianna Madare—you're a rare diamond and the world's greatest best friend. You're my pillar, my secret keeper and my joy.

Roseline 'Wenyasha' Motsi—you carried the dream when I couldn't see it. You were my truth when I didn't believe it was possible. You made it possible.

I love you.